sri lanka &
the philippines

To Reuben, who married me before I learned to cook.

Completely revised and updated in 2011
First published in 1976

This edition published in 2013 by Hardie Grant Books

Hardie Grant Books (Australia)
Ground Floor, Building 1
658 Church Street
Richmond, Victoria 3121
www.hardiegrant.com.au

Hardie Grant Books (UK)
Dudley House, North Suite
34–35 Southampton Street
London WC2E 7HF
www.hardiegrant.co.uk

A Cataloguing-in-Publication entry is available from the catalogue of the National Library of
Australia at www.nla.gov.au
The Complete Asian Cookbook: Sri Lanka & The Philippines
ISBN 978 1 74270 685 6

Publishing Director: Paul McNally
Project Editor: Helen Withycombe
Editor: Ariana Klepac
Design Manager: Heather Menzies
Design Concept: Murray Batten
Typesetting: Megan Ellis
Photographer: Alan Benson
Stylist: Vanessa Austin
Production: Todd Rechner

Colour reproduction by Splitting Image Colour Studio
Printed and bound in China by 1010 Printing International Limited

Find this book on **Cooked.**

THE
Complete
Asian
COOKBOOK

sri lanka & the philippines

CHARMAINE SOLOMON

hardie grant books
MELBOURNE · LONDON

Contents

Foreword

Just as France has its robust country fare as well as its subtle haute cuisine, so too does Asia have a range of culinary delights that can be simple, complex, fiery, mild, tantalising — and compulsive! Not all Asian food is exotic or wildly unusual. Noodle and rice dishes are as commonplace as the pastas and potatoes of the West. Many of the ingredients will be familiar to anyone who knows their way around a kitchen. The main differences have arisen just as they have arisen in other parts of the world — through the use of available ingredients. Thus there is a reliance on some herbs and spices less well known in the West. Meat is often replaced by the nutritious by-products of the soy bean and by protein-rich fish sauces and shrimp pastes.

True, some of the more unusual ingredients take a little getting used to. But once you have overcome what resistance you may have towards the idea of raw fish or dried shrimp paste or seaweed, you'll find that these (and other) ingredients are no less delicious than – and certainly as exciting as – those you use in your favourite dishes.

The introduction will give you a good idea of what to expect in the way of out-of-the-ordinary ingredients. Almost without exception, those called for are readily available in most large supermarkets or Asian grocery stores; in the rare case they are not, suitable substitutes have been given.

Those of you already familiar with Asian cuisine will, I hope, find recipes to interest and excite you in these pages; and I think you will be tempted to explore dishes with which you are less well acquainted. For those of you who are coming to Asian cooking for the first time, I have taken care to make sure the essential steps are clear and precise, with detailed instructions on the following pages for cooking the much-used ingredients (such as rice, noodles, coconut milk and chilli), and pointers on how to joint a chicken, portion fish and select and season a wok.

For most dishes, the names of the recipes have been given in the dominant or most common language or dialect of the country concerned, followed by the English name in italics. Generally, the letter 'a' in Asian words is pronounced as the 'a' in father, never as in cat; the letter 'u' is rather like the 'oo' in look, never as in duty; and the letters 'th' are generally pronounced like an ordinary 't' (slightly aspirated), never as in breath or breathe.

Eating for health

Most Asian food is healthy. Many spices and ingredients such as turmeric, garlic and ginger have proven health-giving properties. However, with today's emphasis on weight control I have made modifications in the quantity and type of fat used for cooking. I have found it is possible to get very good results using almost half the amount of fat called for in many traditional dishes.

In The Philippines, lard is used as a cooking medium. In my kitchen I substitute a light vegetable oil. The flavour will be slightly different, but the way it sits on your stomach will be different too. Coconut oil, used almost exclusively in Sri Lanka and other coconut-growing countries, is now, in its extra-virgin form, considered a healthy oil. If you are battling high cholesterol, when using coconut milk cut down on the quantity and substitute a similar amount of skim milk.

Ghee, or clarified butter, is the main cooking medium in North India and is used in some Sri Lankan dishes. It keeps without refrigeration because it is pure butterfat with all the milk solids removed. It is essential both for flavour and for its ability to reach high temperatures without burning. I use it for flavour, but substitute light oils for a proportion of the ghee.

All of these recipes are adaptable to low-fat diets with very little sacrifice of flavour, since most of the exotic tastes come from herbs, spices and sauces.

Cooking with a wok

If I had to choose one cooking pan to be marooned on a desert island with, I'd choose a wok. It would cope with any kind of food that happened to be available. In it you can boil, braise, fry and steam, and while you can do all these things in pans you already possess, the wok is almost indispensable for the stir-frying technique that many Asian dishes call for. Because of its rounded shape and high, flaring sides you can toss with abandon and stir-fry ingredients without their leaping over the sides; and because the wok is made of thin iron you get the quick, high heat necessary to much Asian cooking.

Though a wok is best used with gas, it is possible to get good results with electricity. Because quick, high heat is required in stir-frying, turn the hotplate on to the highest heat and place the wok directly on it; it is possible to buy woks with a flat base for better contact, or invest in an electric wok where the heating element is built into the pan. The 30–35 cm (12–14 in) wok is most useful. You can cook small quantities in a large wok, but not vice versa.

The wok made of stainless steel is a modern innovation, but a modestly priced iron wok heats up quickly and evenly and, if you remember to dry it well after washing, it will not rust.

Before use, an iron wok must be seasoned. Prepare it by washing thoroughly in hot water and detergent. Some woks, when new, have a lacquer-like coating, which must be removed by almost filling the wok with water, adding about 2 tablespoons bicarbonate of soda (baking soda) and boiling for about 15 minutes. This softens the coating and it can be scrubbed off with a fine scourer. If some of the coating still remains, repeat the process until the wok is free from any lacquer on the inside. To season the new wok, dry it well, put over gentle heat and, when the metal heats up, wipe over the entire inner surface with some crumpled paper towel dipped in peanut oil. Repeat a number of times with more oil-soaked paper until the paper stays clean. Allow to cool. Your wok is now ready for use.

After cooking in it, do not scrub the wok with steel wool or abrasives of any kind. Soak in hot water to soften any remaining food, then rub gently with a sponge, using hot water and detergent – this preserves the surface. Make sure the wok is quite dry, because if moisture stays left in the pan it will rust. Heat the wok gently to ensure complete dryness, then rub over the inside surface with lightly oiled paper. A well-used wok will soon turn black, but this is normal – and the more a wok is used, the better it is to cook in.

Deep-frying

A wok is an efficient pan for deep-frying as it has a wider surface area than a regular frying pan. Be sure that the wok is sitting securely on the stove. Fill the wok no more than two-thirds full and heat the oil over medium heat.

To check the temperature for deep-frying, use a kitchen thermometer if you have one – on average, 180°C (350°F) is the correct temperature. To test without a thermometer, a cube of bread dropped into the oil will brown in 15 seconds at 180°C (350°F), and in 10 seconds if the temperature is 190°C (375°F).

The higher temperature may be suitable to use for foods that don't have great thickness, but if something needs to cook through, such as chicken pieces, use a lower temperature of around 160°C (320°F) – in this case a cube of bread will take nearly 30 seconds to brown. If the temperature is not hot enough, the food will absorb oil and become greasy. If you overheat the oil it could catch fire.

Use refined peanut oil, light olive oil, canola or rice bran oil and lower the food in gently with tongs or a slotted spoon so as not to splash yourself with hot oil. Removing the fried food to a colander lined with crumpled paper towel will help to remove any excess oil.

After cooling, oil may be poured through a fine metal skimmer and stored in an airtight jar away from the light. It may be used within a month or so, adding fresh oil to it when heating. After a couple of uses, it will need to be disposed of properly.

Coconut milk

I have heard many people refer to the clear liquid inside a coconut as 'coconut milk'. I have even read it in books. So, at the risk of boring those who already know, let's establish right away what coconut milk really is. It's the milky liquid extracted from the grated flesh of mature fresh coconuts or reconstituted from desiccated (shredded) coconut.

Coconut milk is an important ingredient in the cookery of nearly all Asian countries. It is used in soups, curries, savoury meat or seafood mixtures and all kinds of desserts. It has an unmistakable flavour and richness and should be used in recipes that call for it.

When the first edition of this book was published in 1975, the only good way to obtain coconut milk outside the countries where coconuts grow was to extract it yourself. These days coconut milk is widely available in tins from supermarkets. Problematically, the quality between brands varies enormously so it is worth comparing a few brands and checking the ingredients list – it should only have coconut and water in it. It should smell and taste fresh and clean and be neither watery nor solid. It is better to avoid brands that include stabilisers and preservatives. Shake the tin well before opening to disperse the richness evenly throughout. Brands in Tetra Paks tend not to be lumpy or watery.

Delicious as it is, coconut milk is full of saturated fat. With this in mind, I suggest that only when coconut cream is required should you use the tinned coconut milk undiluted. Where a recipe calls for thick coconut milk, dilute the tinned product with half its volume in water (for example, 250 ml/8½ fl oz/1 cup tinned coconut milk and 125 ml/4 fl oz/½ cup water). Where coconut milk is required, dilute the tinned coconut milk with an equal amount of water. Where thin coconut milk is required, dilute the tinned coconut milk with two parts by volume of water (for example, 250 ml/8½ fl oz/1 cup tinned coconut milk and 500 ml/17 fl oz/2 cups water).

If you would like to make your own coconut milk, the extraction method is included below. Traditionally, coconut milk is extracted in two stages – the first yield being the 'thick milk', the second extraction producing 'thin milk'. Use a mixture of first and second extracts when a recipe calls for coconut milk unless thick milk or thin milk is specified. Sometimes they are added at different stages of the recipe. Some recipes use 'coconut cream'. This is the rich layer that rises to the top of the thick milk (or first extract) after it has been left to stand for a while.

Making coconut milk from scratch

Using desiccated (shredded) coconut

Makes 375 ml (12½ fl oz/1½ cups) thick coconut milk
Makes 500 ml (17 fl oz/2 cups) thin coconut milk

Many cooks use desiccated coconut for making coconut milk. It is much easier and quicker to prepare than grating fresh coconut, and in curries you cannot tell the difference.

180 g (6½ oz/2 cups) desiccated (shredded) coconut

1.25 litres (42 fl oz/5 cups) hot water

Put the desiccated coconut into a large bowl and pour over 625 ml (21 fl oz/2½ cups) of the hot water then allow to cool to lukewarm. Knead firmly with your hands for a few minutes, then strain through a fine sieve or a piece of muslin (cheesecloth), pressing or squeezing out as much liquid as possible; this is the thick coconut milk.

Repeat the process using the same coconut and remaining hot water. This extract will yield the thin coconut milk. (Because of the moisture retained in the coconut the first time, the second extract usually yields more milk.)

Alternatively, to save time, you can use an electric blender or food processor. Put the desiccated coconut and 625 ml (21 fl oz/2½ cups) of the hot water into the blender and process for 30 seconds, then strain through a fine sieve or piece of muslin (cheesecloth), squeezing out all the moisture. Repeat, using the same coconut and remaining hot water.

Note: Sometimes a richer milk is required. For this, hot milk replaces the water and only the first extract is used. However, a second extract will yield a flavoursome and reasonably rich grade of coconut milk that can be used in soups, curries or other dishes.

Using fresh coconut

Makes 375 ml (12½ fl oz/1½ cups) thick coconut milk
Makes 500 ml (17 fl oz/2 cups) thin coconut milk

In Asian countries, fresh coconut is used and a coconut grater is standard equipment in every household. Grating fresh coconut is easy if you have the right implement for the job. However, if you are able to get fresh coconuts and do not have such an implement, use a food processor to pulverise the coconut and then extract the milk.

1 fresh coconut

1 litre (34 fl oz/4 cups) water or milk

Preheat the oven to 180°C (350°F). Crack the coconut in half by hitting it with the back of a heavy kitchen chopper. Once a crack has appeared, insert the thin edge of the blade and prise it open. Save the sweet liquid inside for drinking. If you do not own a coconut grater, put the two halves on a baking tray and bake in the oven for 15–20 minutes, or until the flesh starts to come away from the shell. Lift it out with the point of a knife and peel away the thin dark brown skin that clings to the white portion. Cut into chunks.

Put the coconut flesh into a food processor with 500 ml (17 fl oz/2 cups) of the water and process until the coconut is completely pulverised. Strain the liquid using a sieve or muslin (cheesecloth) to extract the thick coconut milk. Repeat this process using the same coconut and remaining water to extract the thin milk. Left-over freshly extracted or bought coconut milk may be frozen – ice cube trays are ideal.

Chillies

Fresh chillies are used in most Asian food, particularly that of Southeast Asia. If mild flavouring is required, simply wash the chilli and add it to the dish when simmering, then lift out and discard the chilli before serving. But if you want the authentic fiery quality of the dish, you need to seed and chop the chillies first. To do this, remove the stalk of each chilli and cut in half lengthways to remove the central membrane and seeds – the seeds are the hottest part of the chilli. If you wish to make fiery hot sambals, the chillies are used seeds and all – generally ground or puréed in a food processor.

If you handle chillies without wearing gloves, wash your hands thoroughly with soap and warm water afterwards. Chillies can be so hot that even two or three good washings do not stop the tingling sensation, which can go on for hours. If this happens, remember to keep your hands well away from your eyes, lips or where the skin is especially sensitive. If you have more chillies than you need, they can be wrapped in plastic wrap and frozen, then added to dishes and used without thawing.

Dried chillies come in many shapes and sizes. Generally I use the large variety. If frying them as an accompaniment to a meal, use them whole, dropping them straight into hot oil. If they are being soaked and ground as part of the spicing for a sambal, sauce or curry, first cut off the stalk end and shake the chilli so that the seeds fall out. They are safe enough to handle until they have been soaked and ground, but if you handle them after this has been done, remember to wash your hands at once with soap and water.

Dried chillies, though they give plenty of heat and flavour, do not have the same volatile oils as fresh chillies and so do not have as much effect on the skin.

Rice varieties

One of the oldest grains in the world, and a staple food of more than half the world's population, rice is by far the most important item in the daily diet throughout Asia.

There are thousands of varieties. Agricultural scientists involved in producing new and higher yielding strains of rice will pick differences that are not apparent to even the most enthusiastic rice eater. But, from the Asian consumer's viewpoint, rice has qualities that a Westerner might not even notice – colour, fragrance, flavour, texture.

Rice buyers are so trained to recognise different types of rice that they can hold a few grains in the palm to warm it, sniff it through the hole made by thumb and forefinger, and know its age, variety, even perhaps where it was grown. Old rice is sought after and prized more than new rice because it tends to be fluffy and separate when cooked, even if the cook absent-mindedly adds too much water. Generally speaking, the white polished grains – whether long and fine or small and pearly (much smaller than what we know as short-grain rice) – are considered best.

The desirable features of rice are not the same in every Asian country. In India and Pakistan, Sri Lanka and Burma, fluffy, dry rice is preferred. Long, thin grains are considered best and rice is cooked with salt. The most dreadful thing a cook could do is forget to salt the rice.

Rice is sold either packaged or in bulk. Polished white rice is available as long-, medium- or short-grain. Unpolished or natural rice is available as medium- or long-grain; and in many countries it is possible to buy an aromatic table rice grown in Bangladesh, called basmati rice. In dishes where spices and flavourings are added and cooked with the rice, any type of long-grain rice may be used. In each recipe the type of rice best suited is recommended, but as a general rule, remember that medium-grain or short-grain rice gives a clinging result and long-grain rice, properly cooked, is fluffy and separate.

Preparing rice

To wash or not to wash? Among Asian cooks there will never be agreement on whether rice should be washed or not. Some favour washing the rice several times, then leaving it to soak for a while. Other good cooks insist that washing rice is stupid and wasteful, taking away what vitamins and nutrients are left after the milling process.

I have found that most rice sold in Australia does not need washing but that rice imported in bulk and packaged here picks up a lot of dust and dirt and needs thorough washing and draining.

In a recipe, if rice is to be fried before any liquid is added, the washed rice must be allowed enough time to thoroughly drain and dry, between 30 and 60 minutes. Rice to be steamed must be soaked overnight. Rice for cooking by the absorption method may be washed (or not), drained briefly and added to the pan immediately.

Cooking rice

For a fail-safe way of cooking rice perfectly every time, put the required amount of rice and water into a large saucepan with a tight-fitting lid (see the measures above right). Bring to the boil over high heat, cover, then reduce the heat to low and simmer for 20 minutes. Remove from the heat, uncover the pan and allow the steam to escape for a few minutes before fluffing up the rice with a fork.

Transfer the rice to a serving dish with a slotted metal spoon – don't use a wooden spoon or it will crush the grains. You will notice that long-grain rice absorbs considerably more water than short-grain rice, so the two kinds are not interchangeable in recipes. Though details are given in every rice recipe, here is a general rule regarding proportions of rice and liquid.

Long-grain rice	Short- or medium-grain rice
200 g (7 oz/1 cup) rice use 500 ml (17 fl oz/2 cups) water	220 g (8 oz/1 cup) rice use 375 ml (12½ fl oz/1½ cups) water
400 g (14 oz/2 cups) rice use 875 ml (29½ fl oz/3½ cups) water	440 g (15½ oz/2 cups) rice use 625 ml (21 fl oz/2½ cups) water
600 g (1 lb 5 oz/3 cups) rice use 1.25 litres (42 fl oz/5 cups) water	660 g (1 lb 7 oz/3 cups) rice use 875 ml (29½ fl oz/3½ cups) water
Use 500 ml (17 fl oz/2 cups) water for the first cup of rice, then 375 ml (12½ fl oz/ 1½ cups) water for each additional cup of rice.	Use 375 ml (12½ fl oz/1½ cups) water for the first cup of rice, then 250 ml (8½ fl oz/1 cup) water for each additional cup of rice.

Noodles

There are many different types of noodles available and different Asian countries have specific uses and preferences. Almost all of these varieties are available from large supermarkets or Asian grocery stores.

Dried egg noodles: Perhaps the most popular noodles, these are made of wheat flour. Dried egg noodles must be soaked in hot water for about 10 minutes before cooking. This is not mentioned in the cooking instructions, yet it does make cooking them so much easier – as the noodles soften the strands spread and separate and the noodles cook more evenly than when they are dropped straight into boiling water.

A spoonful of oil in the water prevents boiling over. When water returns to the boil, cook fine noodles for 2–3 minutes and thick noodles for 3–4 minutes. Do not overcook. Drain immediately, then run cold water through the noodles to rinse off any excess starch and cool them so they don't continue to cook in their own heat. Drain thoroughly. To reheat, pour boiling water over the noodles in a colander. Serve with stir-fried dishes or use in soups and braised noodle dishes.

Dried rice noodles: There are various kinds of flat rice noodles. Depending on the type of noodle and thickness of the strands, they have to be soaked in cold water for 30–60 minutes before cooking. Drain, then drop into a saucepan of boiling water and cook for 6–10 minutes, testing every minute after the first 6 minutes so you will know when they are done. As soon as they are tender, drain in a colander and rinse well in cold running water. Drain once more. They can then be fried or heated in soup before serving.

Dried rice vermicelli (rice-stick) noodles: Rice vermicelli has very fine strands and cooks very quickly. Drop into boiling water and cook for 2–3 minutes only. Drain well. Serve in soups or with dishes that have a good amount of sauce. Or, if a crisp garnish is required, use rice vermicelli straight from the packet and deep-fry small amounts for just a few seconds. It will puff and become white as soon as it is immersed in the oil if it is hot enough. Lift out quickly on a slotted spoon or wire strainer and drain on paper towels before serving.

Dried cellophane (bean thread) noodles: Also known as bean starch noodles, these dried noodles need to be soaked in hot water for 20 minutes, then drained and cooked in a saucepan of boiling water for 15 minutes, or until tender. For use as a crisp garnish, deep-fry them in hot oil straight from the packet, as for rice vermicelli (above). In Japan they have a similar fine translucent noodle, known as harusame.

Foreword

Preparing soft-fried noodles

After the noodles have been boiled and drained, spread them on a large baking tray lined with paper towel and leave them to dry for at least 30 minutes – a little peanut oil may be sprinkled over them to prevent sticking. Heat 2 tablespoons each of peanut oil and sesame oil in a wok or large heavy-based frying pan until hot, then add a handful of noodles and cook until golden on one side. Turn and cook the other side until golden, then remove to a plate. Repeat with the remaining noodles. It may be necessary to add more oil to the wok if a large quantity of noodles is being fried, but make sure the fresh oil is very hot first. Serve with beef, pork, poultry or vegetable dishes.

Preparing crisp-fried noodles

Rice vermicelli (rice-stick) and cellophane (bean thread) noodles can be fried in hot oil straight from the packet. Egg noodles need to be cooked first, then drained and spread out on a large baking tray lined with paper towel to dry for at least 30 minutes – a little peanut oil can be sprinkled over them to prevent sticking. Heat sufficient peanut oil in a wok or heavy-based frying pan over medium heat. When the oil is hot, deep-fry the noodles, in batches, until crisp and golden brown. Drain on paper towel. These crisp noodles are used mainly as a garnish.

Preparing whole chickens

Jointing a chicken

I have often referred to cutting a chicken into serving pieces suitable for a curry. This is simply cutting the pieces smaller than joints so that the spices can more readily penetrate and flavour the meat.

To joint a chicken, first cut off the thighs and drumsticks, then separate the drumsticks from the thighs. Cut off the wings and divide them at the middle joint (wing tips may be added to a stock but do not count as a joint). The breast is divided down the centre into two, then across into four pieces – do not start cooking the breast pieces at the same time as the others, but add them later, as breast meat has a tendency to become dry if cooked for too long.

A 1.5 kg (3 lb 5 oz) chicken, for instance, can be jointed, then broken down further into serving pieces. The thighs are cut into two with a heavy cleaver; the back is cut into four pieces and used in the curry, though not counted as serving pieces because there is very little meat on them. Neck and giblets are also included to give extra flavour.

Preparing whole fish

Cutting fish fillets into serving pieces

Fish fillets are of varying thickness, length and density. For example, whole fillets of flathead can be dipped in batter and will cook in less than a minute in hot oil, whereas a fillet of ling or trevalla will need to be cut into 3 cm (1¼ in) strips for the same recipe.

Let common sense prevail when portioning fish fillets, but always remember that fish is cooked when the flesh turns opaque when flaked with a fork or knife.

Cutting fish steaks into serving pieces

Depending on the size of the fish, each steak may need to be cut into four, six or eight pieces. Once again, smaller portions are better, for they allow flavours to penetrate and you can allow more than one piece per person. The accompanying sketch shows how to divide fish steaks – small ones into four pieces, medium-sized ones into six pieces and really large steaks into eight pieces.

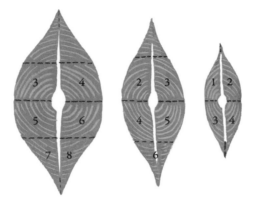

Foreword

Sri Lanka

I was born and lived most of my unmarried life in this small, beautiful tropical island, shaped like a tear–drop and situated at the southernmost tip of the Indian subcontinent so that it has been romantically called 'the pearl in the ear of India'.

It has been known by many names at different times, for it is an ancient land and its recorded history goes back to 483 BC, when Vijaya, a prince of the lion race (Sinhalas) set foot on the island. Some of the names by which it has been called during its 2500 years of recorded history are Taprobane, Simundu, Salike, Sila-diva, Serendib, Zeilan and Ceylon.

Roloff Beny, in his delightful book, *Island: Ceylon*, writes, 'In Sinhala, the language of the majority of the inhabitants, it is reverently known as Sri Lanka, or "Resplendent Island", but I myself prefer the name given to it by the first travellers from China, which in translation is, "The Land Without Sorrow"'.

I had been away for a number of years when I revisited Sri Lanka for the purpose of writing this book. It was with a small shock that I realised all over again just how beautiful a land it is. Driving along the coast road one is surrounded by greens and blues and golden hues; languid, swaying coconut palms, the Indian Ocean incredibly blue and green and even purple in patches; sandy beaches that go on for mile after smooth, golden mile. Both sea and air are so warm that there is no chill either entering the water or leaving it. And there are no sharks because the island is surrounded by protective coral reefs, so it is a skin-diver's paradise.

Within less than a hundred miles you can travel from the coast to the central hills where, 2000 metres (6000 feet) above sea level, the air is cool and crisp and the natural vegetation includes conifers and pines; here, English and Scottish planters grew the best tea in the world and felt at home in the cool, misty climate. On the coastal plains there is a year-round temperature of 32°C (90°F) and city dwellers seek the comfort of air-conditioned buildings.

In spite of its tiny size, Sri Lanka boasts an amazing variety of food and styles of cooking. The island has a rich heritage of indigenous dishes and its regional cooking is strongly individual and varied. For example, Kandyan Sinhalese cooking, with its emphasis on hill country vegetables and fruits; coastal cooking, making the best of the seafood with which the land is blessed; Tamil cooking, closely linked to that of southern India, and which is especially prevalent in Jaffna, in the north.

In Sri Lanka, as in any other country, the most typical food is cooked in the villages – getting precise recipes is almost impossible. They don't cook by a book. A pinch of this, a handful of that, a good swirl of salty water; taste, consider, adjust seasoning. That's the way Sinhalese women cook, and no two women cook exactly alike. Even using the same ingredients, the interpretation of a recipe is completely individual. Ask a cook how much of a certain ingredient she uses and she'll say, 'This much,' showing you with her hand. Spoon measures would be looked upon as an affectation. You watch, make notes and try to achieve the same results by trial and error. And when you arrive at the correct formula, write it down for posterity.

In addition to regional characteristics, some of the most popular dishes reflect influences from other lands. After a hundred years or so it does not matter that this or that style of cooking was introduced by foreigners who came and stayed, either as traders or conquerors – Indians, Arabs, Malays, Moors, Portuguese, Dutch and British. The dishes they contributed have been adapted to local ingredients, but retain their original character. They are not presented as Sinhalese dishes but accepted and enjoyed as part of the richly varied cuisine. The influence of the Muslims and Malays is responsible for the use of certain flavourings such as saffron and rosewater and the spicy korma, pilau and biriani which are Sri Lankan only by adoption.

When the Portuguese ruled Sri Lanka for 150 years in the sixteenth and seventeenth centuries, they left behind words that have worked their way into the language and customs that are very much a part of rural and urban life. Many recipes end with an instruction to 'temper' the dish. This comes from the Portuguese word, *temperado*, which means to fry and season. The Portuguese also contributed a number of sweetmeats that remain popular. These are served at celebrations (Sri Lankans are enthusiastic about celebrating every happy occasion) and people take enormous pride in old family recipes, which they guard with jealous care.

Then came the Dutch, and though their rule ended after a mere 138 years, their descendants stayed on in this prosperous land. They too brought with them recipes laden with butter and eggs in true Dutch tradition, but in the spice-rich land of their adoption they took on new flavours of cardamom, cinnamon, cloves, nutmeg and mace. The traditional Christmas cake (see page 112) is a fine example of this, a fruit cake which stands above all others for flavour and richness.

My father's family trace their ancestry back to the Dutch settlers. One early memory is of my paternal grandmother making preserves in an enormous brass pan that shone like gold. She was famous for her preserves, chutneys and jellies, and regularly won gold medals at the annual show. I have never seen anyone so meticulous about cooking.

Then I remember preparations for Christmas, always a time of much cooking and tasting. Eggs were bought by the hundred, not the dozen. And why not? The Christmas cake would require fifty egg yolks and a breudher (Dutch yeast cake) twenty more. When the egg vendor appeared it was the signal for the servants of the household to bring large basins of water to the veranda where grandmother sat to make her purchases. Into these the egg seller would put the eggs. Any that floated or bobbed about uncertainly were disqualified and only those that sank sedately to the bottom, signifying freshness, were considered worthy. The cooking of traditional foods was a family affair, and everyone had their part.

Serving and eating a Sri Lankan meal

Rice is the staple food of the people of Sri Lanka and has been adopted by all the communities (except, perhaps, the die-hard British). When enquiring whether one has had a meal, the literal translation of the question as asked in the Sinhalese language is, 'Have you eaten rice?' And all over the island the midday meal is rice and curry, Sinhalese-style.

For such a meal everything is put on the table at once – rice, fish and meat curries, soup, vegetables and accompaniments. It is perfectly correct to have a serving of everything on your plate at one time. Soup may be ladled over the rice or sipped from a cup between mouthfuls, but it is not the first course. The meal can be eaten with the fingers as the people of the country do, or use a spoon and fork, which is widely accepted now except on special occasions such as the Sinhalese New Year, when everybody goes traditional and eats with their fingers.

Desserts are unknown except on festive occasions, and the meal usually ends with some of the luscious fruit so plentiful on the island: mangoes of at least a dozen different varieties; papayas so sweet they seem to have been macerated in honey; bananas in even greater variety than mangoes; mangosteens and rambutan in season; avocados which are served with cream and sugar; and the huge, ungainly jak fruit, spiky green outside and the size of a large watermelon, with large, golden, fleshy seed pods of overwhelming sweetness and distinctive flavour.

Curries are not necessarily classified according to the main ingredients, but according to the type of spicing, the method of cooking, or the colour which, to the initiate, conveys a whole lot more than just whether a curry is white, red or black. White curries are based on coconut milk and are usually mild and have a lot of liquid so they double as soups. Red curries are based on few spices and a large amount of chilli powder or ground chillies that give the curry its vivid colour and red hot flavour. (In Sri Lanka it is quite commonplace to have as many as thirty large dried red chillies to spice a dish for six to eight people. Unless you are accustomed to spices on a grand scale, tread warily. Use some chilli for flavour and paprika to achieve the desired colour. Discretion is by far the better part of valour!) Black curries are the most typical curries in Sri Lanka. They get their dark colour because the coriander, cumin and fennel are roasted until a rich coffee brown. This dark-roasting brings out nuances of flavour in a subtle and wholly pleasant way, making the cooking of this little island strongly individual. If buying curry powder for use in Sri Lankan recipes, look for a label that says 'Ceylon Curry Powder' and if this is not obtainable, use the recipe opposite if you wish to duplicate the true flavour. Or, if using individual spices, always toast the coriander, cumin and fennel separately in a dry frying pan until dark brown before using.

Utensils

Cooking in true native style is always done on stone or brick hearths over wood fires. I remember Josie, a genial, round-faced, motherly woman who was the family cook for so many years that she addressed me as 'baby' (as the youngest member of the family is called) even when I was married and with babies of my own. Josie presided over the 'big kitchen' with its huge fireplaces, blowing through a piece of hollow metal tubing to get more heat out of the fire, stirring her clay chatties (cooking pots) with coconut shell spoons, and producing some of the best meals I have ever eaten. She had no time for the 'small kitchen' where the mistress of the house cooked on a gas range or baked cakes in the oven. Everything Josie wanted to cook could be made to her satisfaction in the time-honoured way, using the most primitive equipment. Like every other cook in the land she awoke before dawn to make the breakfast specialities, and each day, before she started to cook, she would grind her spices. This is done on a rectangular grinding stone the size of a pillow, using another stone shaped like a bolster. In Western kitchens, a powerful food processor does this job.

While a stone mortar and pestle can be used for grinding whole spices for curries, an electric spice grinder is far quicker. Having one means you can always have freshly ground spices, which have a better flavour. There is something about food cooked in clay chatties, especially curries, that is rather special. It is as though the clay absorbs and then gives out again the character of the food cooked in it. So though a chatty costs a mere few cents, when a cook gets used to a certain pot she is not easily parted from it. Most cooks keep special chatties for meat, others for fish and yet others for vegetables. However, a set of heavy-based saucepans is very suitable for curry cooking, and one with a well-fitting lid for cooking rice.

In place of the coconut shell spoons used for stirring, use wooden spoons. In curry cooking, metal spoons are not recommended. And keep these special curry spoons only for curries, or they may transmit the strong flavours they absorb to other dishes. There is no special equipment you need for the recipes in this book, except if you wish to try the Appe (hoppers, page 24) and even then you can make do with an omelette pan if you cannot find the proper curved iron pan used to make these rice pancakes. A wok is not suitable, as the metal is too thin and gets too hot.

Your Sri Lankan shelf

black mustard seeds

cardamom, pods and ground

Ceylon curry powder (below)

chilli, powder and whole dried red chillies

cinnamon, sticks and ground

cloves, whole and ground

coconut milk (pages 8–9)

coriander, seeds and ground

cumin, seeds and ground

curry leaves, fresh or dried

dried prawn (shrimp) powder

dried shrimp

fennel, seeds and ground

fenugreek, seeds

ghee

kencur (aromatic ginger) powder

lemongrass

Maldive fish (smoked dried tuna)

palm sugar (jaggery)

pandanus leaf

paprika

peppercorns, whole black

tamarind pulp

turmeric, ground

vegetable oil or coconut oil

Ceylon curry powder

In Sri Lankan (Ceylonese) cooking, one of the main characteristics is that the spices are dark-roasted. This gives them an aroma completely different from Indian curries. So be sure to use curry powder that is labelled 'Ceylon curry powder'. If you cannot buy it ready-made, here is a simple recipe.

165 g (6 oz/1 cup) coriander seeds

60 g (2 oz/½ cup) cumin seeds

1 tablespoon fennel seeds

1 teaspoon fenugreek seeds

5 cm (2 in) cinnamon stick

1 teaspoon whole cloves

1 teaspoon cardamom seeds

2 tablespoons dried curry leaves

2 teaspoons chilli powder (optional)

2 tablespoons rice flour (optional)

In a dry frying pan over low heat, individually roast the coriander seeds, cumin seeds, fennel seeds and fenugreek seeds, stirring constantly until each one becomes a fairly dark brown – do not let them burn.

Place the roasted spices into an electric spice grinder or use a mortar and pestle. Break the cinnamon stick into small pieces and grind with the cloves, cardamom and curry leaves until you have a fine powder. Add the chilli powder and rice flour, if using. Store in an airtight jar for up to 3 months.

Breads, Rice and Snacks

◆

Rotis

Flatbread

Serves: 6–8

Similar to Indian flatbreads, Sri Lankan rotis contain fresh grated coconut or, in its absence, desiccated (shredded) coconut. Serve with curries and sambols. It is a popular breakfast in Sri Lanka.

300 g (10½ oz/2 cups) roti flour or plain (all-purpose) flour

45 g (1½ oz/½ cup) desiccated (shredded) coconut

1 teaspoon salt

ghee or oil for cooking

Mix together the flour, coconut and salt in a bowl. Add just enough water to form a soft dough, about 250 ml (8½ fl oz/1 cup). Knead the dough until it forms a ball and does not stick to the side of the bowl. Rest the dough for about 30 minutes.

Shape the dough into balls, approximately the size of a golf ball. Pat each one out to a circle.

Lightly grease a large heavy-based frying pan or griddle plate with ghee over low heat and cook the rotis on both sides until lightly browned on both sides. Serve hot.

Breads, Rice and Snacks ◆

Leila's Rotis
Leila's flatbread

Makes: about 6

When my daughter Deborah and I travelled around Asia to research for the *Complete Asian Cookbook*, we stayed with my old friend and first mentor, Anne Abayasekara. Anne had given me my first job as a 19-year-old, straight out of school. Throwing me in at the deep end, she told me to write a weekly cookery column. 'But I don't know how to cook,' I wailed. 'Then you had better learn,' she replied with scant sympathy. Fortunately, I had the right contacts. My aunts were excellent cooks and supplied me with a wealth of recipes.

Leila was Anne's family cook at the time of our visit. Leila's rotis were a great treat, with the zing of some fresh chillies and finely chopped fresh red Asian shallots, which are used widely in Sri Lanka. I thought they were too good not to include here.

350 g (12½ oz/2 cups) rice flour or 300 g (10½ oz/2 cups) roti flour or plain (all-purpose) flour

1 teaspoon baking powder

45 g (1½ oz/½ cup) freshly grated or desiccated (shredded) coconut

2 teaspoons salt

2 teaspoons butter or coconut oil

2 tablespoons finely chopped red Asian shallots

1 tablespoon finely chopped fresh red or green chilli

1 egg, beaten

ghee or oil for cooking

Mix together the flour, baking powder, coconut and salt in a bowl. Rub in the butter until evenly distributed, then add the shallots, chilli, egg and just enough water to form a stiff dough, about 250 ml (8½ fl oz/1 cup). Knead the dough until it forms a ball and does not stick to side of the bowl. Rest the dough for about 30 minutes.

Shape the dough into balls, approximately the size of a golf ball. Pat each one out to a circle.

Lightly grease a large heavy-based frying pan or a griddle plate with ghee over low heat and cook the rotis on both sides until lightly browned on both sides. Serve hot.

Iddi Appe
Stringhopper pilau

Serves: 8–10

Stringhoppers get their name because they are composed of fine 'strings' of dough forced through a perforated mould to form lacy circles about the size of a saucer. These are steamed on woven round rattan racks piled over each other – they are light, fluffy and dry to the touch. An average serving is about six or eight stringhoppers served for breakfast with a simple Coconut milk gravy (page 88) and Coconut sambol (page 100). Stringhoppers are also a favourite at festive lunches or dinners and in this setting are shredded finely and cooked as pilau, accompanied by Scrambled eggs with flavourings (page 84), Frikkadels (page 82), meat or chicken curry and Chilli sambol (page 101). They are typical of Sri Lankan food, but since making them can be an arduous task, the recipe that follows is a substitute using Chinese rice vermicelli (rice-stick) noodles. I call it 'mock stringhopper pilau'.

500 g (1 lb 2 oz) rice vermicelli (rice-stick) noodles

100 g (3½ oz) ghee

3 large onions, thinly sliced

10 curry leaves

½ teaspoon ground saffron or 1 teaspoon saffron strands

1 teaspoon ground turmeric

1 teaspoon ground cardamom

4–5 hard-boiled eggs, peeled and sliced, to serve

155 g (5½ oz/1 cup) cooked peas, to serve

40 g (¼ cup) cashew nuts or almonds, toasted, to serve

Cook the rice vermicelli noodles in a saucepan of salted boiling water for 2 minutes only. Drain well.

Heat the ghee in a large saucepan over medium heat. Add the onion and curry leaves and cook until the onion is golden. Add the saffron, turmeric and cardamom and stir well. Add the rice vermicelli and toss the ingredients together until mixed through and evenly coloured. Season to taste with salt and pepper. Serve garnished with the eggs, peas and nuts.

Note

If liked, the hard-boiled eggs can be rubbed with ground turmeric and fried in a little hot oil until golden.

Kiri Bath
Milk rice

Serves: 4–5

A simple preparation of rice cooked in coconut milk, kiri bath is part of the traditions of the Sinhalese people. It is a 'must' on New Year's Day, and on the first day of each month it is the accepted breakfast dish. It is usually served with hot sambols, but some prefer it with grated palm sugar (jaggery). Don't expect long fluffy grains with a hint of coconut when you cook this dish. Rich with creamy coconut and dense enough to cut with a knife, for my family it is a once-a-year treat.

440 g (15½ oz/2 cups) short-grain rice

500 ml (17 fl oz/2 cups) thick coconut milk (pages 8–9)

2 teaspoons salt

1 cinnamon stick (optional)

Wash the rice well and drain in a colander.

Put the rice and 750 ml (25½ fl oz/3 cups) water into a saucepan and bring to the boil. Reduce the heat to low, cover, and cook for 15 minutes. Add the coconut milk, salt and cinnamon stick, if using, stir well with the handle of a wooden spoon, then re-cover the pan and continue to cook over low heat for a further 10–15 minutes, or until all the milk has been absorbed. Remove from the heat, discard the cinnamon. Cool slightly, then turn out onto a flat plate. Mark off in diamond shapes and serve with Coconut sambol (page 100).

Ghee Rice

Serves: 4–5

400 g (14 oz/2 cups) basmati or other long-grain rice

50 g (1¾ oz) ghee

1 large onion, thinly sliced

4 whole cloves

6 cardamom pods, bruised

1 cinnamon stick

875 ml (29½ fl oz/3½ cups) beef, chicken or mutton stock

2 teaspoons salt

Wash the rice well and drain in a colander for 30 minutes.

Heat the ghee in a saucepan over medium heat. Add the onion and cook until golden. Add the spices and rice and cook, stirring constantly with a slotted metal spoon, for 5 minutes. Add the hot stock and salt and bring to the boil, then reduce the heat to low, cover, and cook for 15–20 minutes without lifting the lid. Remove from the heat, uncover and rest for 5 minutes to allow steam to escape. Gently fluff up the rice with a fork, removing the whole spices.

When transferring the rice to a serving dish, use a slotted metal spoon to avoid crushing the grains of rice. Serve hot, accompanied by curries of meat and vegetables, pickles and sambols.

Kaha Bath
Yellow rice

Serves: 6–8

This is a special-occasion dish in which the rice is cooked in coconut milk and delicately flavoured with spices.

600 g (1 lb 5 oz/3 cups) long-grain rice

80 g (2¾ oz) ghee

2 onions, thinly sliced

6 whole cloves

20 whole black peppercorns

12 cardamom pods, bruised

1½ teaspoons ground turmeric

3½ teaspoons salt

12 curry leaves

1 stem lemongrass

1 pandanus leaf (optional)

1.25 litres (42 fl oz/5 cups) thin coconut milk (pages 8–9)

Wash the rice well and drain in a colander for 30 minutes.

Heat the ghee in a large saucepan over medium heat. Add the onion and cook until it begins to turn golden. Add the cloves, peppercorns, cardamom pods, turmeric, salt, curry leaves, lemongrass and pandanus leaf, if using. Add the rice and cook, stirring constantly, for 2–3 minutes, or until the rice is well coated. Add the coconut milk and bring to the boil, then reduce the heat to low, cover, and cook for 20–25 minutes without lifting the lid.

When the rice is cooked, the spices will have risen to the top. Remove the spices and the leaves. Fluff up the rice lightly with a fork. Serve hot, accompanied by Fried pork curry (page 65) or other curries and accompaniments.

Koppe Bath
Cup rice

Serves: 8

1 quantity Yellow rice (above)

1 quantity Coconut sambol (page 100)

4 hard-boiled eggs, peeled and halved (optional)

Basically, this is yellow rice moulded in a cup, with a layer of coconut sambol in the centre. You can put a halved hard-boiled egg in the base of the cup before half filling with the warm rice if you like. Press firmly. Cover this with 1 tablespoon of coconut sambol, then cover with more yellow rice. Again press down firmly, then turn out onto a serving dish. Repeat until all the rice is used up. Serve with curries and accompaniments.

Appe
Hoppers

Makes: about 20

The name doesn't really tell you anything unless you've been in this part of the world and eaten *appe*, *appam* or 'hoppers' as they are variously called. They are bowl-shaped pancakes made from a batter of rice flour, yeast and coconut milk, swirled in hemispherical pans (rather like a smaller, more acutely curved wok) and baked over hot coals with more coals heaped on the lid. They can be cooked with equal success on gas or electric stoves, and the pans are sold in shops that specialise in utensils from India and Sri Lanka. I have also made them in a small omelette pan – the shape is unorthodox but the taste is perfect. In Sri Lanka, hoppers are served for breakfast, but are equally good as a snack any time.

My husband, Reuben, was the hopper king and his recipe became the Sunday morning favourite for our grandchildren. Ever in search of the perfect formula, this is the final version, dated 24 November 2006, written in his own hand in our kitchen copy of an earlier edition of this cookbook. For health reasons he used water instead of coconut milk, but if you prefer, use 190 ml (6½ fl oz/¾ cup) thin coconut milk instead of the second amount of water.

---

2 teaspoons dried yeast

2 teaspoons sugar

40 g (1½ oz/¼ cup) ground rice

130 g (4½ oz/¾ cup) rice flour

110 g (4 oz/¾ cup) self-raising flour

1 teaspoon salt

extra-virgin coconut oil for cooking

Variation

To make biththara appe (egg hoppers), proceed as for hoppers, but as soon as the pan is coated with batter, break a fresh egg into the centre. Cover and cook as before – the egg will cook to just the right stage while the hopper bakes, and looks prettier than an egg cooked any other way. Serve with salt and pepper for seasoning.

You can also make miti kiri appe (coconut cream hoppers) served with sweet accompaniments such as fresh grated coconut and palm sugar (jaggery). If to be served sweet, spoon a small amount of rich coconut milk into the centre before putting on the lid.

Sprinkle the yeast into a bowl with 190 ml (6½ fl oz/¾ cup) lukewarm water, stir to dissolve, then add the sugar and set aside for 10 minutes, or until the mixture starts to froth. This is to test whether the yeast is live. If it does not froth start again with a fresh batch of yeast.

Put the ground rice, rice flour, self-raising flour and salt into a large bowl. Add the yeast mixture to 190 ml (6½ fl oz/¾ cup) water (or use thin coconut milk) and stir into the dry ingredients to form a smooth, thick batter. Allow to stand in a warm (turned off) oven for 1 hour, or until the mixture rises and doubles in size – the batter should be of a thick pouring consistency, but thin enough to cover the side of the pan with an almost translucent coating when the batter is swirled. It may be necessary to add some extra water or thin coconut milk. A little practice will tell you when you have achieved the perfect consistency, and so much depends on the absorbency of the flour that it is not possible to give an exact measurement – aim for the consistency of pouring (single/light) cream.

Lightly oil a hopper pan over low heat, pour in a small ladleful of the batter and immediately swirl the pan so that the batter coats the pan two-thirds of the way up. Cover the pan (any saucepan lid that fits just inside the top edge will do) and cook over very low heat for about 5 minutes, or until the upper edges begin to turn a pale toasty colour – the batter will run down the sides to the centre to create a little circle of spongy mixture, much like a crumpet, while the curved edge is very thin, crisp and wafer-like. Remove to a wire rack and repeat with the remaining mixture, oiling the pan as needed. Serve the hoppers warm, accompanied by Coconut sambol (page 100) and Lunu miris sambola (page 100) or any kind of meat, fish or chicken curry.

Lampries
Curry parcels

Serves: 16–18

Just as biriani is the ultimate in festival meals in India, lampries is *the* special-occasion dish in Sri Lanka. If you are invited to a meal in a Sri Lankan home and lampries are served, you are being honoured. The name comes from the Dutch word, *lomprijst*, and it is a fascinating combination of rice cooked in stock, Dutch-style forcemeat balls, Sinhalese curries and sambols, all wrapped in banana leaves and baked. Each component recipe can be made ahead, some may even be frozen, to make 'lampries wrapping day' as easy as possible.

On a recent visit to Sri Lanka, I was treated to a lampries lunch. On opening the parcel, I was reminded of the type of rice traditionally used in this festive dish, the small, pearly grains of *muttu samba*. This rice is highly regarded in that country, but my husband did not like it because it is parboiled, giving it a distinct flavour which was not to his taste. Without apologies I have therefore used basmati rice.

---

banana leaves

3 quantities Ghee rice (page 22)

1 quantity Lampries curry (page 66)

1 quantity Frikkadels (page 82)

1 quantity Eggplant pickle (page 89)

1 quantity Chilli sambol (page 101)

1 quantity Prawn blacan (page 85)

thick coconut milk (pages 8–9)

Note

It is practical to make a large number of lampries, as they are ideal for parties. They freeze well and can be kept frozen for 2 months. Heat in a moderate oven from frozen state for 40 minutes, or 20 minutes if first thawed in the refrigerator. If you can't get banana leaves, use 40 cm (16 in) squares of foil instead.

Using large, wide banana leaves, strip them from the centre rib and cut into pieces, approximately 30–40 cm (12–16 in) long. Wash and dry with a clean tea towel (dish towel) and heat over a gas flame for a few seconds on each side to make them pliable so they will fold without splitting. Alternatively, put the banana leaves in a large basin or sink and pour boiling water over the top.

Preheat the oven to 190°C (375°F).

On each banana leaf, place 1 cup firmly-packed ghee rice and arrange 2 tablespoons lampries curry, 2 frikkadels, 2 teaspoons eggplant pickle, 1 teaspoon chilli sambol and 1 heaped teaspoon prawn blacan around the rice. Pour 2 tablespoons thick coconut milk over the rice. Fold the banana leaf over and fasten with short bamboo skewers or fold over the foil to make a neat rectangular package. Some people prefer to enclose leaf parcels in foil as well – this is a good idea in case the leaf splits while heating or serving.

Heat the lampries for about 20–25 minutes, then remove from the oven and arrange on a large serving tray. When the lampries are opened, the fragrance of the food is unbelievably appetising. Allow 1–2 lamprics for each guest. A bowl of chilled Cucumber sambol (page 96) can be served alongside.

Pittu
Steamed coconut and rice flour bread

Serves: 8

Pittu is a combination of flour and freshly grated coconut steamed in a bamboo steamer. The resulting roll, looking something like a white suet pudding but infinitely lighter in texture, is served with fresh coconut milk, hot sambols and curries, and is especially popular as a breakfast dish. To improvise a steamer, use a tall, narrow tin, such as a biscuit (cookie) or coffee tin, cut away the base, make a dozen holes in the lid and invert the tin so the lid is now the base. Fill the tin with the coconut mixture. If a steamer is not available, put the cylinder in a large saucepan with a trivet in it to hold the tin above the water level.

110 g (4 oz/2 cups) grated fresh coconut
or 180 g (6½ oz/2 cups) desiccated
(shredded) coconut and 250 ml
(8½ fl oz/1 cup) water

150 g (5½ oz/1 cup) plain (all-purpose) flour
or 175 g (6 oz/1 cup) rice flour

125 g (4½ oz/1 cup) fine semolina

1½ teaspoons salt

If using desiccated coconut, put it into a large bowl, sprinkle with the water and use your fingertips to work gently together until the coconut is moist. Fresh coconut does not need water.

Add the sifted flour, semolina and salt to the coconut and rub gently with the fingertips until the mixture resembles fine crumbs. Fill a bamboo or metal cylinder with this and press down lightly. Steam over boiling water for 10–15 minutes. Allow to cool slightly, then unmould and serve with coconut milk for moistening, Ground onion and chilli sambol (page 100) or a hot curry such as Tripe curry (page 62), which is traditional with pittu. Pittu can also be served with sweet accompaniments such as coconut milk, grated palm sugar (jaggery) or sugar.

Patties

Makes: about 75 patties

Birthdays are celebrated with much enthusiasm in Sri Lanka and these popular savoury pastries are a 'must' for parties. The traditional pastry used for patties is a rather unusual one that uses coconut milk. You can also use a shortcrust pastry, if you prefer.

Patty pastry

300 g (10½ oz/2 cups) plain (all-purpose) flour

½ teaspoon salt

1 tablespoon beef dripping or butter

60 ml (2 fl oz/¼ cup) thick coconut milk (pages 8–9)

2 egg yolks, beaten

oil for frying

Filling

500 g (1 lb 2 oz) chicken thighs

500 g (1 lb 2 oz) beef rump steak or lamb leg chops

250 g (9 oz) pork chops

125 g (4½ oz) bacon or ham

20 g (¾ oz) ghee

1 onion, finely chopped

8 curry leaves

2 teaspoons Ceylon curry powder (page 17)

1 teaspoon ground turmeric

¼ teaspoon ground cloves

½ teaspoon ground cinnamon

½ teaspoon freshly ground black pepper

2 teaspoons salt

1 stem lemongrass, bruised, or 2 strips lemon zest

125 ml (4 fl oz/½ cup) thick coconut milk (pages 8–9)

2 tablespoons finely chopped fresh dill

4–6 hard-boiled eggs, peeled and chopped

1 egg white

coconut oil or vegetable oil for deep-frying

To make the patty pastry, sift the flour and salt into a bowl and rub in the dripping with your fingertips. Add the combined coconut milk and egg yolk and knead lightly to a smooth dough. If necessary add a little extra milk or flour – flour varies in absorbency and it is difficult to be absolutely precise. Wrap the dough in baking paper and refrigerate for 30 minutes. Take one-quarter of the dough at a time and roll out very thinly on a lightly floured work surface. Use an 8 cm (3¼ in) pastry cutter to make about 75 circles in total.

To make the filling, put the chicken, beef and pork into a saucepan with just enough water to cover. Bring to the boil, then reduce the heat to low, cover, and simmer for 20 minutes. Remove from the heat and strain, reserving 375 ml (12½ fl oz/1½ cups) of the stock. Remove the meat from the bones, discarding the bones, and cut the chicken, beef and pork into dice. Remove the rind from the bacon and cut into small squares.

Heat the ghee in a saucepan over medium heat. Add the onion and curry leaves and cook until the onion starts to brown. Add the curry powder, turmeric, cloves, cinnamon, pepper and salt and stir well. Add the reserved stock, lemongrass and the diced meat.

Mix well, cover, and simmer gently until the meats are tender and the liquid has almost evaporated. Add the coconut milk and dill, stir and cook uncovered until the coconut milk has been absorbed. Remove from the heat, discarding the lemongrass and curry leaves.

Place 1 teaspoonful of filling in the centre of each pastry round. Top with a piece of hard-boiled egg, then wet the edges of the pastry with egg white, fold over to make a half circle and press the edges firmly together to seal. In Sri Lanka, the edge is always ornamented by pressing with the tines of a fork. Repeat until all the pastry has been filled.

Heat the oil in a large heavy-based saucepan over medium heat. When the oil is hot, deep-fry the patties, in batches, until golden. Drain on paper towel and serve warm.

Mas Paan
Meat buns

Makes: about 30

Popular as a snack at any time of day, yeast buns filled with curried meat are sold piping hot from the oven at almost every tea boutique in Sri Lanka. You may need to break the beef cubes in the beef curry down slightly to fit the buns.

This dough recipe is the rising agent in Breudher (the Sri Lankan yeast cake on page 108). The extra gluten helps it to rise and hold its shape.

1 quantity Beef curry (page 56)

500 g (1 lb 2 oz) potatoes, peeled and diced

1 egg yolk, beaten with 1 tablespoon water

Basic dough

125 ml (4 fl oz/½ cup) milk

3 teaspoons sugar

2 teaspoons salt

90 g (3 oz) butter

30 g (1 oz) compressed yeast or 2 teaspoons active dried yeast

900 g (2 lb/6 cups) plain (all-purpose) flour

1 tablespoon gluten flour

Add the potato to the beef curry during the final 30 minutes of cooking and cook the curry until it is very dry. Remove from the heat and allow to cool.

To make the dough, put the milk into a saucepan over high heat and bring almost to the boil, then remove from the heat, stir in sugar, salt and butter and allow to cool to lukewarm.

Put the yeast in a bowl, pour over 375 ml (12½ fl oz/1½ cups) water and stir until dissolved. Add the lukewarm milk mixture and sift in 450 g (1 lb/3 cups) of the plain flour and the gluten flour. Beat with a wooden spoon until smooth. Add just enough of the remaining flour to make a soft dough.

Turn the dough out onto a lightly floured work surface and knead for about 10 minutes, or until smooth and elastic. Shape into a smooth ball and place into a greased bowl. Cover with a clean tea towel (dish towel) and set aside in a warm draught-free place for about 1 hour, or until doubled in size. The dough is now ready to be divided and rolled for use.

To prepare the buns, knock back the dough and divide into 30 equal portions – this is probably easiest if you divide the dough first into 3 equal portions, then each of those into 5, then each of the 5 portions in half. Flatten each portion into a circle and place a spoonful of the meat and potato curry in the centre. Bring the edges together, pressing and moulding to seal. Buns should be nicely rounded on top and not too doughy at the bottom – to achieve this keep the dough thicker in the centre of the rounds and thin at the edges.

Arrange the buns, seam side down, on greased baking trays, with enough space between to allow for rising and spreading. Cover with a clean tea towel and leave in a warm place for 30–40 minutes or until nearly doubled in size.

Preheat the oven to 200°C (400°F). Brush the egg glaze over the top and bake for 15–20 minutes, or until golden brown. Serve hot or cold.

Sri Lankan Pan Rolls

Makes: about 25

These most delicious pancake rolls are a speciality of Thelma Koch and her daughter, Pax Crowe. Perfect finger food, they may be made ahead and frozen, then heated before serving.

1 tablespoon vegetable oil

1 large brown onion, finely chopped

3 garlic cloves, finely chopped

2 rashers (slices) bacon (optional)

10 curry leaves, chopped

1 tablespoon Ceylon curry powder (page 17)

500 g (1 lb 2 oz) minced (ground) beef

1 large potato, peeled and cut into 1 cm (½ in) dice

1 tablespoon lemon or lime juice

1 tablespoon Worcestershire sauce

1 teaspoon sugar

1 teaspoon salt

1 tablespoon finely chopped ginger

1 tablespoon chopped fresh dill

1 teaspoon freshly ground black pepper

Pancakes

300 g (10½ oz/2 cups) plain (all-purpose) flour

1 teaspoon baking powder

5 eggs

500 ml (17 fl oz/2 cups) milk

1 teaspoon salt

1 teaspoon sugar

1 tablespoon melted butter or oil

200 g (7 oz/2 cups) dry breadcrumbs

oil for deep-frying

Heat the oil in a saucepan over medium heat and fry the onion, garlic, bacon and curry leaves until soft. Stir in the curry powder. Add the beef and cook over high heat until it browns. Add the potato, lemon or lime juice, Worcestershire sauce, sugar, salt, ginger and 125 ml (4 fl oz/½ cup) water. Cover, and cook over medium heat until the potato is cooked through and the liquid has been absorbed – the mixture should be moist, not wet. Finally, add the dill and pepper. Taste and adjust the seasoning if needed – you may like to add a teaspoon of chilli powder or chopped fresh chilli. This filling may be made beforehand and refrigerated. Allow to cool as it is easier to work with a cold filling.

To make the pancakes, sift together the flour and baking powder in a bowl. Whisk 3 of the eggs in a separate mixing bowl. Alternately add the flour and milk, then add the salt, sugar and melted butter or oil and beat until smooth – the batter should be just thick enough to coat the back of a spoon. If necessary, thin out with a little extra milk or water. Set aside to rest for 1 hour.

Lightly oil a small pancake pan and place over medium heat. Pour in enough batter to make a pancake with a 14 cm (5½ in) diameter. When cooked on one side, remove to a plate and start cooking the next pancake. While it cooks, place a tablespoon of filling on the cooked pancake. Fold in the two sides and then roll up like a spring roll. Move to a tray and continue making, filling and rolling the pancakes.

When all the mixture has been used and the pancakes are rolled, dip each one in the remaining beaten eggs and roll in dry breadcrumbs to coat – the rolls may be refrigerated at this stage.

To serve, fry the rolls in moderately hot oil, then drain on paper towel and serve plain or with chilli sauce. These rolls also freeze well. Thaw, then heat in a moderate oven when required.

Seafood

Malu Curry
Fish curry

Serves: 4–6

....

4 large fish steaks, such as Spanish
   mackerel, mulloway or cod

1 teaspoon freshly ground black pepper

1 teaspoon salt

1 teaspoon ground turmeric

oil for frying

½ tablespoon tamarind pulp

2 onions, finely chopped

½ teaspoon fenugreek seeds

2 garlic cloves, thinly sliced

1 teaspoon finely chopped fresh ginger

1 small cinnamon stick

1 pandanus leaf

8 curry leaves

1½ tablespoons Ceylon curry powder
   (page 17)

500 ml (17 fl oz/2 cups) coconut milk
   (pages 8–9)

Wipe the fish with damp paper towel. Rub each fish steak with a mixture of the pepper, salt and turmeric. Heat the oil in a wok or large heavy-based frying pan over medium heat. When the oil is hot, cook the fish to a golden colour on both sides. Drain on paper towel and set aside.

Soak the tamarind pulp in 60 ml (2 fl oz/¼ cup) hot water for 10 minutes. Squeeze to dissolve the pulp in the water, then strain, discarding the seeds and fibre. Set aside.

Heat 2 tablespoons of oil in a large saucepan over low heat. Add the onion, fenugreek seeds, garlic and ginger and cook until they turn golden. Add the cinnamon stick, pandanus leaf, curry leaves and curry powder and cook for 2 minutes, stirring regularly. Add the tamarind liquid and coconut milk and simmer, uncovered, until the sauce has thickened and slightly reduced. Add the fish steaks and spoon over the sauce; continue to simmer for about 10 minutes. Serve hot with rice and vegetable curries.

Kiri Malu
Fish white curry

Serves: 6

500 g (1 lb 2 oz) skinless, boneless, firm white fish fillets

½ teaspoon ground turmeric

1 teaspoon salt

1 teaspoon fenugreek seeds

1 onion, thinly sliced

2 garlic cloves, finely chopped

8 curry leaves

375 ml (12½ fl oz/1½ cups) thin coconut milk (pages 8–9)

125 ml (4 fl oz/½ cup) thick coconut milk (pages 8–9)

lemon juice, to taste

Wipe the fish with damp paper towel. Rub each fish fillet with turmeric and ½ teaspoon of the salt. Soak the fenugreek seeds in 60 ml (2 fl oz/¼ cup) water for 30 minutes.

Put the fenugreek seeds into a saucepan with the onion, garlic, curry leaves, thin coconut milk and the remaining salt. Simmer gently until the onion has softened, stirring well. Add the fish and simmer for a further 10 minutes, then add the thick coconut milk and cook for a few minutes longer. Remove from the heat and add the lemon juice to taste. Serve with rice and sambols.

Ambul Thiyal
Sour curry of fish

Serves: 6

In Sri Lanka, the acid element traditionally used in fish curries is *goraka*, a bright orange fruit that is divided into segments and dried. The dried segments are almost black. If you can obtain this ingredient, use four segments and grind them to a pulp. I have used tamarind as a substitute because it is more readily available.

500 g (1 lb 2 oz) skinless, boneless, firm white fish fillets, such as snapper

1 tablespoon tamarind pulp

60 ml (2 fl oz/¼ cup) vinegar

1 onion, finely chopped

3 garlic cloves, finely chopped

1 teaspoon finely grated fresh ginger

1 teaspoon salt

6–8 curry leaves

1 stem lemongrass, bruised, or 2 strips lemon zest

2.5 cm (1 in) cinnamon stick

¼ teaspoon fenugreek seeds

¼ teaspoon freshly ground black pepper

¼ teaspoon chilli powder (optional)

2 tablespoons oil

Wipe the fish with damp paper towel. Cut each fish fillet into large pieces. Soak the tamarind pulp in the vinegar for 10 minutes. If the tamarind is very dry, heat the vinegar and tamarind in an enamel saucepan for a few minutes, adding some water. When cool enough to handle, squeeze to dissolve the pulp in the water, then strain, discarding the seeds and fibre.

Put the fish, tamarind liquid and remaining ingredients into a large heavy-based frying pan with 375 ml (12½ fl oz/1½ cups) water and bring to the boil. Reduce the heat to low and simmer until the fish is cooked through and the sauce has thickened – shake the pan or turn the fish pieces carefully once or twice during cooking. Serve with rice.

Note

Because of the high acid content of this curry, it is preferable to use a non-reactive enamel or stainless steel pan.

Seafood

Thakkali Malu
Fish curry with tomato

Serves: 4–5

....

500 g (1 lb 2 oz) fish steaks, such as
  kingfish, tuna, Spanish mackerel or
  mullet

1 teaspoon ground turmeric

1 teaspoon salt, plus extra to taste

oil for frying

1 large onion, roughly chopped

3 garlic cloves

2 teaspoons finely chopped fresh ginger

1 ripe tomato, chopped

1 tablespoon Ceylon curry powder
  (page 17)

1 teaspoon chilli powder

500 ml (17 fl oz/2 cups) thin coconut milk
  (pages 8–9)

Wipe the fish with damp paper towel. Cut each fish fillet
into large pieces. Rub each fish steak with the turmeric
and salt.

Heat the oil in a large heavy-based frying pan over low heat.
Add the fish and cook on both sides until golden brown.
Drain on paper towel.

Put the onion, garlic, ginger and tomato in a food processor
and process to a smooth paste.

Heat 2 tablespoons of oil in a saucepan over medium heat.
Add the tomato mixture and cook for 3–4 minutes, or until
the oil begins to separate. Add the curry powder and chilli
powder, coconut milk and about 1 teaspoon salt, and bring
to the boil. Simmer for a few minutes, then add the fish to
the sauce and simmer for 10 minutes. Serve with rice and
your favourite accompaniments.

Malu Bola Cutlis
Fish koftas

Makes: about 60

425 g (15 oz) tinned mackerel or snoek

500 g (1 lb 2 oz) floury potatoes, peeled

1 large onion, finely chopped

1 large or 2 small eggs, beaten

80 g (2¾ oz/1 cup) fresh white breadcrumbs

2 teaspoons salt

½ teaspoon freshly ground black pepper

1 teaspoon Ceylon curry powder (page 17)

1 tablespoon finely chopped fresh dill

2 teaspoons finely chopped fresh red or green chillies

dry breadcrumbs or cornflake crumbs for coating

oil for deep-frying

Drain the fish, pressing with a spoon to get rid of as much liquid as possible.

Cook the potatoes in a saucepan of boiling water until cooked through, then mash while hot. Measure and take same weight as that of the drained fish. Mix the mackerel and potato together in a bowl with the onion, egg, fresh breadcrumbs, salt, pepper, curry powder, dill and chilli and mix well to combine. Shape the mixture into small balls – you should make about 60 in total. Roll each ball in the dry breadcrumbs to coat, then place on baking trays and refrigerate for 1 hour to help set the coating.

Heat the oil in a large heavy-based saucepan over medium heat. When the oil is hot, deep-fry the balls, in batches, until brown. Do not have the oil too hot or the crumb coating will float off and the koftas will brown before they are heated through. When nicely brown lift out with a slotted spoon and drain on paper towel. These fish koftas can be made ahead of time and frozen in a plastic freezer bag when cool – you will need to reheat in a moderate oven before serving.

Malu Roast
Spicy barbecued fish

Serves: 4

4 × 500 g (1 lb 2 oz) small whole tailor
  or mullet

2 tablespoons lemon juice

1½ teaspoons salt

1 teaspoon ground turmeric

¼ teaspoon freshly ground black pepper

1 small onion, sliced

2 garlic cloves, peeled

2 slices fresh ginger

¼ teaspoon ground cinnamon

¼ teaspoon ground cloves

8 curry leaves, crushed (optional)

1 tablespoon ground coriander

1 teaspoon ground cumin

1 teaspoon chilli powder, or to taste

1 tablespoon oil

banana leaves or foil for wrapping

Clean and scale the fish, leaving the head on. Wipe inside the fish cavity with damp paper towel that has first been dipped in coarse salt. Trim any long spines or fins neatly. Cut diagonal slashes in the flesh with a sharp knife, about 2.5 cm (1 in) apart, and rub each fish with a little of the lemon juice, salt, turmeric and pepper.

Put all the remaining ingredients into a food processor and process to a smooth paste (or use a mortar and pestle). Rub the mixture all over each fish, making sure it is pushed well into the slashes and body cavity. Spoon any remaining mixture over the fish and wrap each fish in banana leaves or foil to make a neat parcel. Put over glowing coals or under a preheated grill (broiler) and cook for 10 minutes on each side. Open the parcel for the last few minutes of cooking to evaporate any excess moisture. Serve hot with rice.

Siyambala Malu Curry
Fish curry with tamarind

Serves: 6

500 g (1 lb 2 oz) fish steaks, such as bonito, tuna or mackerel

1 tablespoon tamarind pulp

1½ tablespoons Ceylon curry powder (page 17)

1 teaspoon salt

¼ teaspoon ground turmeric

1 teaspoon chilli powder

60 ml (2 fl oz/¼ cup) oil

8 curry leaves

¼ teaspoon fenugreek seeds

1 onion, finely chopped

2 garlic cloves, finely chopped

Wipe the fish with damp paper towel. Cut each fish fillet into large pieces. Soak the tamarind pulp in 125 ml (4 fl oz/ ½ cup) hot water for 10 minutes. Squeeze to dissolve the pulp in the water, then strain, discarding the seeds and fibre.

Combine the tamarind liquid with the curry powder, salt, turmeric and chilli powder and pour over the fish in a bowl. Leave to marinate for 20 minutes.

Heat the oil in a large heavy-based frying pan over medium heat. Add the curry leaves and fenugreek seeds and cook for 2 minutes, then add the onion and garlic, and continue to cook until the onion is golden, stirring occasionally. Add the fish and marinade, cover, and cook over low heat for 10 minutes, or until the fish is opaque and flakes easily when tested with a fork. Serve with rice and vegetable curries.

Rathu Isso Curry
Red prawn curry

Serves: 6

750 g (1 lb 11 oz) small raw prawns (shrimp)

1 onion, finely chopped

3 garlic cloves, finely chopped

1 teaspoon finely grated fresh ginger

1 small cinnamon stick

¼ teaspoon fenugreek seeds

3 curry leaves

1 small stem lemongrass, bruised, or 2 strips lemon zest

1 pandanus leaf

½ teaspoon ground turmeric

1½ teaspoons chilli powder

2 teaspoons paprika

1 teaspoon salt

500 ml (17 fl oz/2 cups) thin coconut milk (pages 8–9)

lemon juice, to taste

With kitchen scissors, snip off the prawn feelers; leave the heads and shells on. (In Sri Lanka prawns are often cooked in their shells for better flavour.) Put all the ingredients, except the lemon juice, into a large saucepan and bring slowly to simmering point. Simmer, uncovered, for 20 minutes, or until the onion has softened and the prawns are cooked through. Stir in the lemon juice, to taste, and season with salt if needed. Serve hot with rice.

Seafood

Isso Thel Dhala
Dry-fried prawns

Serves: 6

Once again, paprika comes to the rescue and makes this spicy prawn preparation an enticing red colour. If you are inclined to try it the real Sri Lankan way, increase the amount of chilli powder ... but don't say I didn't warn you!

60 ml (2 fl oz/¼ cup) oil

2 large onions, finely chopped

2 garlic cloves, finely chopped

2 teaspoons salt

1 teaspoon chilli powder, or to taste

2 teaspoons paprika

¼ teaspoon ground turmeric

2 teaspoons pounded Maldive fish (smoked dried tuna) or dried prawn powder

1 kg (2 lb 3 oz) raw prawns (shrimp), peeled and deveined, tails left intact

2 teaspoons sugar

1 tablespoon tomato paste (concentrated purée)

Heat the oil in a large heavy-based frying pan over medium heat. Add the onion and garlic and cook over low heat until the onion is golden brown. Add the salt, chilli powder, paprika and turmeric and cook for 1 minute, then add the Maldive fish and prawns, and stir-fry for 3 minutes. Add 125 ml (4 fl oz/½ cup) water, cover, and simmer for 5 minutes. Stir in the sugar and tomato paste and cook for a few minutes further, until the sauce is a dark reddish brown, thick and dry enough to coat the prawns. Serve with rice.

Note

As an appetiser, these prawns are delicious served on small squares of fried bread.

Kakuluwo Omlet Curry

Crab omelette curry

Serves: 2–4

A simple omelette served in curry sauce is no longer commonplace, and when it is a crab omelette the result is something to remember ... and I do. My father was not what you would call a domesticated man, but he had one culinary accomplishment: he could make a crab omelette better than any other I ever tasted. Dad would go to the market and choose himself the biggest, heaviest, freshest crab he could find and bring it home, still alive and bent on escape. When it had been steamed to flavoursome succulence and the meat was carefully extracted from the shell and claws, Dad combined eggs, crab, spring onion (scallion) and fresh chilli to create a masterpiece. He never did write down his recipe, but I have managed to reconstruct something very like it. Do try to use fresh crabmeat – it is a vast improvement on the frozen or tinned varieties. Serve as an omelette or in a curry sauce.

4 eggs, lightly beaten

salt and freshly ground black pepper

175 g (6 oz/1 cup) flaked crabmeat

lemon juice, to taste

20 g (¾ oz) butter

3 spring onions (scallions), thinly sliced

1 fresh green or red chilli, deseeded and finely chopped

2 tablespoons finely chopped fresh dill (optional)

1 quantity Vegetable curry sauce (page 69)

Season the egg with ½ teaspoon salt and a good grinding of black pepper. Season the crabmeat with salt and pepper to taste, and add a squeeze of lemon juice.

Heat the butter in a large heavy-based frying pan or omelette pan over low heat. Add the spring onion and chilli and cook until soft, stirring frequently. Pour in the egg and stir in the dill, then start scraping portions of egg from the side of the pan and letting the uncooked egg run out to the edges. When set and golden on the bottom and creamy on top, spoon the heated crabmeat down the centre of the omelette and fold over once. Spoon the warm vegetable curry sauce over the top and serve hot with rice.

Kakuluwo Curry
Crab curry

Serves: 4–6

....

2 large raw or cooked mud crabs

3 onions, finely chopped

6 garlic cloves, finely chopped

2 teaspoons finely grated fresh ginger

½ teaspoon fenugreek seeds

10 curry leaves

8 cm (3¼ in) cinnamon stick

1–2 teaspoons chilli powder

1 teaspoon ground turmeric

3 teaspoons salt

1 litre (34 fl oz/4 cups) thin coconut milk
    (pages 8–9)

2 tablespoons desiccated (shredded)
    coconut

1 tablespoon ground rice

500 ml (17 fl oz/2 cups) thick coconut milk
    (pages 8–9)

1 tablespoon lemon juice

Remove the large shells from the crabs and discard the fibrous tissue under the shell. Divide each crab into 4 portions, breaking each body in half and separating the claws from the body, leaving the legs attached. Crack the claws with the back of a heavy knife or cleaver.

Put the onion, garlic, ginger, fenugreek seeds, curry leaves, cinnamon stick, chilli powder, turmeric, salt and thin coconut milk into a large saucepan, cover and simmer over medium–low heat for 30 minutes. Add the crab – if using raw crabs, continue to simmer for a further 20 minutes, or 5–7 minutes if cooked crabs are used. The crab should be submerged in the sauce during cooking. Remove the crab to a plate.

Meanwhile, heat the coconut and ground rice in a separate dry frying pan over medium heat, stirring constantly, until golden brown. Transfer to a food processor, add half of the thick coconut milk and process until well combined. Add to the pan with the remaining coconut milk and the lemon juice, simmer for 10 minutes, then return the crab to the pan and heat through. Serve with rice.

Note

If the onions are large and tough, first soften by cooking gently in 2–3 tablespoons oil for 20 minutes before including in the recipe.

Dhallo Badun
Fried squid curry

Serves: 4–6

1 kg (2 lb 3 oz) squid

2 onions, thinly sliced

4 garlic cloves, thinly sliced

2 teaspoons finely grated fresh ginger

1 teaspoon ground turmeric

1 teaspoon chilli powder (optional)

2 tablespoons Ceylon curry powder
  (page 17)

½ teaspoon fenugreek seeds

1 cinnamon stick

1 stem lemongrass or 2 strips lemon zest

10 curry leaves

60 ml (2 fl oz/¼ cup) vinegar

750 ml (25½ fl oz/3 cups) coconut milk
  (pages 8–9)

1½ teaspoons ghee or oil

Clean each squid, removing the ink sac and discarding the head. Rinse the tubes under cold running water to remove the skin. Drain well and cut the tubes into rings.

Place in a deep saucepan with all the remaining ingredients except the ghee. Bring to the boil, then reduce the heat to low and simmer for about 1 hour, or until the squid is tender and the sauce has reduced and thickened. Remove from the heat.

Remove the squid from the sauce. In a separate saucepan, heat the ghee over medium–high heat and cook the squid. Add the sauce to the fried squid and simmer for 1–2 minutes to heat through. Serve with rice and sambols.

Poultry

Kukul Gujura Curry
Chicken gizzard curry

Serves: 6

Gizzards are the secondary stomach of poultry. After slow and careful cooking they change to a melting texture similar to lamb shanks. If available, duck gizzards may also be used for this recipe.

750 g (1 lb 11 oz) chicken gizzards

1½ tablespoons ground coriander

3 teaspoons ground cumin

80 ml (2½ fl oz/⅓ cup) oil

2 onions, finely chopped

5 garlic cloves, finely chopped

1 tablespoon finely chopped fresh ginger

1 teaspoon chilli powder

½ teaspoon ground turmeric

½ teaspoon ground fenugreek (optional)

2 ripe tomatoes, chopped

1½ teaspoons salt

2 tablespoons chopped fresh coriander
(cilantro) leaves

Wash and clean the gizzards, removing any yellow membrane, and leave to drain in a colander.

Put the ground coriander in a small dry frying pan and stir over low heat for a few minutes until roasted to a fairly dark brown and giving out a pleasant aroma. Remove to a plate. Roast the cumin in the same way.

Heat the oil in a large heavy-based saucepan over medium heat. Add the onion, garlic and ginger and cook until the onion softens and starts to turn golden brown. Add the chilli powder, turmeric, fenugreek, if using, and roasted coriander and cumin and continue cooking for 1 minute, then add the tomato and salt and stir well. Add the chicken gizzards and stir until they are well coated with the spice mixture. Add 750 ml (25½ fl oz/3 cups) hot water and simmer over low heat for 2 hours, or until the gizzards are tender. Sprinkle with the coriander leaves, stir to combine, and cook for a further 5 minutes. Serve hot with rice.

Kukul Mas Curry
Chicken curry

Serves: 4–5

In this recipe, paprika is used to give the required red colour – in Sri Lanka the colour is achieved by using about 30 dried red chillies!

1.5 kg (3 lb 5 oz) whole chicken or chicken leg and thigh quarters

3 tablespoons ghee or oil

¼ teaspoon fenugreek seeds (optional)

10 curry leaves

2 large onions, finely chopped

4–5 garlic cloves, finely chopped

2 teaspoons finely grated fresh ginger

1 teaspoon ground turmeric

1 teaspoon chilli powder

1 tablespoon ground coriander

1 teaspoon ground cumin

½ teaspoon ground fennel

2 teaspoons paprika

2 teaspoons salt

2 tablespoons malt vinegar

2 tomatoes, peeled and chopped (see note)

6 cardamom pods, bruised

1 cinnamon stick

1 stem lemongrass, bruised, or 2 strips lemon zest

250 ml (8½ fl oz/1 cup) thick coconut milk (pages 8–9)

lemon juice, to taste

Joint the chicken – cut the breast and thighs in half, leaving the wings and drumsticks whole.

Heat the ghee in a large heavy-based saucepan over low heat. Add the fenugreek seeds, if using, and the curry leaves and cook until they start to brown. Add the onion, garlic and ginger and cook until the onion is golden. Add the turmeric, chilli powder, coriander, cumin, fennel, paprika, salt and vinegar and stir well to combine.

Add the chicken to the pan and stir until it is well coated in the spices. Add the tomato, whole spices and lemongrass, cover, and cook over low heat for 40–50 minutes, or until the chicken is tender. Add the coconut milk, taste and add more salt and a squeeze of lemon juice, if desired. Do not cover after adding coconut milk. Serve with rice and accompaniments.

Note

The easiest way to peel a tomato is to first loosen the skin. This can be done by scoring a cross in the base of each tomato and blanching them briefly in a saucepan of boiling water. When cool, use your fingers to peel away the skins.

Thara Padre Curry
Duck padre curry

Serves: 6–8

The name of this curry has always fascinated me. Why it is called 'padre' curry is not clear. It contains arrack, or whisky, and one explanation offered is that it was a favourite with the padre because it was his only opportunity to imbibe!

2 × 1.7 kg (3 lb 12 oz) whole ducks

2 large onions, chopped

6 garlic cloves, chopped

1½ tablespoons finely chopped fresh ginger

2 tablespoons Ceylon curry powder (page 17)

1 cinnamon stick

2 pandanus leaves

1 stem lemongrass, bruised, or 2 strips lemon zest

750 ml (25½ fl oz/3 cups) coconut milk (pages 8–9)

2 teaspoons salt

60 ml (2 fl oz/¼ cup) vinegar

60 ml (2 fl oz/¼ cup) arrack or whisky

1 tablespoon soft brown sugar

2 tablespoons ghee or oil

Cut the ducks into portions. Put in a large heavy-based saucepan with all the remaining ingredients except the ghee, arrack and sugar. Bring to the boil, then reduce the heat to low, cover, and simmer until the duck is tender, about 1½–2 hours. Remove from the heat, remove the duck pieces from the sauce and drain.

Heat the ghee in a separate saucepan over medium heat. Add the duck and cook until golden, pouring off any excess oil. Add the sauce, arrack and sugar, and simmer for a further 10 minutes. Serve with plain rice or Ghee rice (page 22), Fried onion sambol (page 97) and Cucumber sambol (page 100). For a variation, garnish with slices of lightly fried potato.

Meat

Jaggery Satay
Beef with palm sugar

Serves: 6

Sweet, sour, salty, hot: this meat preparation is all of the above, but does not use any of the curry spices. A spicy sauce may be served with it if liked, but is not strictly necessary. Without palm sugar (jaggery) the flavour will not be exactly right, but soft brown sugar can be substituted.

750 g (1 lb 11 oz) round (topside), blade (chuck) or other lean steak

2 tablespoons tamarind pulp

2 teaspoons chilli powder, or to taste

½ teaspoon freshly ground black pepper

½ teaspoon salt, or to taste

45 g (1½ oz/¼ cup) chopped palm sugar (jaggery) or 2 tablespoons soft brown sugar

80 ml (2½ fl oz/⅓ cup) oil

Cut the beef into 2 cm (¾ in) cubes. Soak the tamarind pulp in 250 ml (8½ fl oz/1 cup) hot water for 10 minutes. Squeeze to dissolve the pulp in the water, then strain, discarding the seeds and fibre. Add the chilli powder, pepper, salt and palm sugar to the tamarind liquid and stir to dissolve the sugar.

Heat the oil in a small frying pan over medium heat. When the oil is hot, cook the beef, in batches, for about 1-2 minutes, or until the cubes are lightly browned. Remove the beef with a slotted spoon and transfer to a saucepan. Wait until the oil stops spitting, then repeat until all the beef has been cooked.

Pour the tamarind mixture over the beef in the saucepan and bring to the boil, then reduce the heat to low, cover, and simmer until the beef is tender and the sauce has reduced. Thread the meat onto skewers and serve with white rice.

Harak Mas Curry

Beef curry

Serves: 8–10

1.5 kg (3 lb 5 oz) stewing steak

1 tablespoon ghee or oil

2 large onions, finely chopped

1 tablespoon finely chopped fresh ginger

3–4 garlic cloves, finely chopped

4 tablespoons Ceylon curry powder
  (page 17)

1 teaspoon ground turmeric

2 teaspoons black mustard seeds

2 teaspoons salt

1 tablespoon vinegar

2 fresh red chillies, deseeded and chopped

3 ripe tomatoes, peeled and chopped

Cut the steak into 5 cm (2 in) cubes.

Heat the ghee in a saucepan over low heat. Add the onion, ginger and garlic and cook until just starting to turn golden. Add the curry powder, turmeric and mustard seeds and cook for 2–3 minutes, stirring regularly. Add the salt, vinegar and beef and stir well to coat. Add the chilli and tomato, cover, and simmer for about 2 hours, or until the sauce has thickened. Serve with rice and other accompaniments. If the sauce is too thin when the meat is tender, cook over high heat, stirring frequently, until reduced.

Kuruma Iraichchi
Beef pepper curry

Serves: 8

1 kg (2 lb 3 oz) lean stewing steak

2 teaspoons salt

2–4 teaspoons freshly ground black pepper

1 tablespoon ground coriander

2 teaspoons ground cumin

1 teaspoon ground fennel

½ teaspoon ground turmeric

2 onions, finely chopped

3 garlic cloves, finely chopped

1½ teaspoons finely grated fresh ginger

2 fresh red chillies, deseeded and sliced

8 curry leaves

2 pandanus leaves

1 stem lemongrass or 2 strips lemon zest

2 tablespoons vinegar

500 ml (17 fl oz/2 cups) thin coconut milk
   (pages 8–9)

1 tablespoon ghee or oil

250 ml (8½ fl oz/1 cup) thick coconut milk
   (pages 8–9)

Cut the meat into 5 cm (2 in) cubes and beat lightly with a meat mallet. Season the beef with the salt and pepper and toss to coat.

Separately roast the coriander, cumin and fennel in a dry frying pan. Add the roasted coriander to the beef and set aside the cumin and fennel.

Put the meat into a saucepan with the turmeric, onion, garlic, ginger, chilli, curry leaves, pandanus leaves, lemongrass, vinegar and thin coconut milk. Bring to the boil, then reduce the heat to low, cover, and simmer until the meat is tender. If the sauce thickens too quickly add a little water. Remove the meat from the sauce using a slotted spoon.

Heat the ghee in a separate frying pan and cook the beef for a few minutes, stirring often.

Add the cumin and fennel to the thick coconut milk and mix into the sauce in the pan, then return the meat to the sauce and continue to simmer, uncovered, over low heat, until the sauce has thickened. Serve with rice and other accompaniments.

Mas Ismoru
Beef smoore

Serves: 6–8

This recipe features a large piece of beef, cooked in a spicy coconut milk mixture, then sliced like a roast beef and served with plenty of rich, thick gravy spooned over. Serve with rice or Rotis (page 19) and Fried onion sambol (page 97).

1.5 kg (3 lb 5 oz) silverside or round steak (in one piece)

2 onions, finely chopped

6 garlic cloves, finely chopped

1 tablespoon finely chopped fresh ginger

1 cinnamon stick

10 curry leaves

1 stem lemongrass or 2 strips lemon zest

3 tablespoons Ceylon curry powder (page 17)

½ teaspoon fenugreek seeds

125 ml (4 fl oz/½ cup) vinegar

½ pickled lime or lemon (page 92)

500 ml (17 fl oz/2 cups) thin coconut milk (pages 8–9)

1 teaspoon ground turmeric

2 teaspoons chilli powder, or to taste

2 teaspoons salt, or to taste

250 ml (8½ fl oz/1 cup) thick coconut milk (pages 8–9)

50 g (1¾ oz) ghee

Pierce the meat all over with a skewer and put in a large saucepan with all the ingredients except the thick coconut milk and ghee. Cover and simmer gently for 1½–2 hours, or until the meat is tender. Add the thick coconut milk and cook, uncovered, for a further 15 minutes. Remove the meat to a serving dish and, if the gravy is too thin, reduce by boiling rapidly. Transfer the gravy to a bowl.

Heat the ghee in the cleaned pan over low heat. Add the beef and brown on all sides, then return the gravy to the pan and heat through. To serve, slice the meat and arrange on a platter with the gravy served separately.

Satay Curry
Skewered beef curry

Serves: 6

750 g (1 lb 11 oz) rump steak, cut into cubes

½ teaspoon ground turmeric

½ teaspoon freshly ground black pepper

½ teaspoon salt

20 thin slices fresh ginger

20 thin garlic slices

60 g (2 oz) ghee or 60 ml (2 fl oz/¼ cup) oil

¼ teaspoon fenugreek seeds

8 curry leaves

2 onions, finely chopped

3 garlic cloves, finely chopped

1 teaspoon finely grated fresh ginger

1 tablespoon ground coriander, dry-roasted

2 teaspoons ground cumin, dry-roasted

½ teaspoon chilli powder

½ teaspoon ground fennel, dry-roasted

½ teaspoon kencur (aromatic ginger) powder

¼ teaspoon ground cardamom

a pinch of ground cloves

1 teaspoon salt

625 ml (21 fl oz/2½ cups) coconut milk (pages 8–9)

Cut 10 bamboo skewers into 10 cm (4 in) lengths and soak in water to prevent them from burning. Sprinkle the beef with the turmeric, pepper and salt and mix well to combine. Thread the beef onto the skewers alternately with the ginger and garlic slices.

Heat the ghee in a heavy-based frying pan over high heat. Add the skewers and cook, in batches, turning to seal on all sides. Remove to a plate.

Add the fenugreek seeds and curry leaves to the pan and cook for 1 minute, then add the onion, garlic and ginger and cook until the onion is golden. Add the coriander, cumin, chilli powder and fennel and cook for 1 minute longer, stirring well, then add the remaining ingredients and simmer, uncovered, until thick and smooth. If necessary add more water or coconut milk. Return the skewered beef to the pan, spoon over the sauce and simmer for a further 20 minutes or until the meat is tender. Serve with white rice or ghee rice and other accompaniments.

Peegodu Curry
Diced liver curry

Serves: 4

500 g (1 lb 2 oz) calves' livers, sliced

10 whole black peppercorns

1 teaspoon salt

1 tablespoon ghee or oil

1 onion, finely chopped

3 garlic cloves, finely chopped

1 teaspoon finely chopped fresh ginger

1 stem lemongrass or 2 strips lemon zest

¼ teaspoon ground cloves

½ teaspoon freshly ground black pepper

½ teaspoon ground cinnamon

8 curry leaves

60 ml (2 fl oz/¼ cup) vinegar

500 ml (17 fl oz/2 cups) coconut milk (pages 8–9)

2 tablespoons chopped fresh dill

Rinse the liver and drain, then place into a small saucepan with enough water to cover.

Add the peppercorns and salt and cook for about 15 minutes, or until the liver is firm. Remove from the heat, allow to cool, then cut the liver into very small dice.

Heat the ghee in the cleaned pan over medium heat. Add the onion, garlic and ginger and cook until the onion softens. Add all the remaining ingredients, return the liver to the pan, and cook, uncovered, until the sauce has thickened.

Babath Curry
Tripe curry

Serves: 6

1 kg (2 lb 3 oz) honeycomb tripe

8 large dried red chillies

2 teaspoons ground cumin

½ teaspoon ground turmeric

½ teaspoon fenugreek seeds

½ teaspoon kencur (aromatic ginger)
   powder

8 curry leaves

1 stem lemongrass, bruised, or 2 strips
   lemon zest

1 pandanus leaf

8 whole cardamom pods

4 whole cloves

1 small cinnamon stick

2 onions, finely chopped

4 garlic cloves, finely chopped

1½ teaspoons finely grated fresh ginger

500 ml (17 fl oz/2 cups) thin coconut milk
   (pages 8–9)

1½ teaspoons salt

250 ml (8½ fl oz/1 cup) thick coconut milk
   (pages 8–9)

2 tablespoons lemon juice

Wash the tripe well and cut into 5 cm (2 in) squares.

Soak the chillies (stalks and seeds removed) in 125 ml
(4 fl oz/½ cup) hot water for 10 minutes. Put the chillies
and their soaking water into a food processor and process
until puréed.

Put the tripe, chilli purée and all the remaining ingredients,
except the thick coconut milk and lemon juice, into a large
saucepan and bring to the boil. Reduce the heat to low,
cover, and simmer for 1½ hours, or until the tripe is tender
and the sauce has thickened. Add the thick coconut milk
and simmer, uncovered, for 10 minutes, stirring regularly.
Remove from the heat, add the lemon juice and serve with
rice or Pittu (page 27).

Ooroomas Rathu Curry
Pork red curry

Serves: 8

1 kg (2 lb 3 oz) pork belly

8–10 large dried red chillies

1 tablespoon tamarind pulp

½ teaspoon ground turmeric

2 onions, 1 roughly chopped and
   1 thinly sliced

5 garlic cloves

1½ teaspoons chopped fresh ginger

5 cm (2 in) cinnamon stick

2 teaspoons salt

1 stem lemongrass or 2 strips lemon zest

10 curry leaves

¼ teaspoon fenugreek seeds

1 pandanus leaf (optional)

125 ml (4 fl oz/½ cup) thick coconut milk
   (pages 8–9)

1 tablespoon oil or melted ghee

2 tablespoons lemon juice

Cut the pork into 5 cm (2 in) cubes and put into a saucepan. Remove the stalks and seeds from the dried chillies and soak them in 190 ml (6½ fl oz/¾ cup) hot water for 10 minutes. Soak the tamarind pulp in 125 ml (4 fl oz/½ cup) hot water for 10 minutes. Squeeze to dissolve the pulp in the water, then strain, discarding the seeds and fibre.

Put the chillies and their soaking water into a food processor with the turmeric, chopped onion, garlic and ginger and process until smooth. Add to the pork in the pan, along with the cinnamon stick and tamarind liquid. Add the salt, half of the lemongrass, half of the curry leaves, half of the fenugreek seeds and half of the pandanus leaf, if using. Bring to the boil, then reduce the heat to low, cover, and simmer until the pork is tender. Add the coconut milk and simmer, uncovered, for a further 10 minutes.

Heat the oil in a separate saucepan over medium heat. Add the sliced onion and the remaining lemongrass, curry leaves, fenugreek seeds and pandanus leaf. When the onion is golden, add the pork mixture and lemon juice, stir to combine, and simmer over low heat for about 5 minutes. Serve with rice and accompaniments.

Ooroomas Badun
Fried pork curry

Serves: 6–8

If you like a rich, oily curry, use pork belly. Use pork neck for a leaner version of this dish.

1 kg (2 lb 3 oz) pork belly or neck, cut into cubes

1 tablespoon tamarind pulp

1 tablespoon oil

10 curry leaves

¼ teaspoon fenugreek seeds (optional)

2 onions, finely chopped

4 garlic cloves, finely chopped

1½ teaspoons finely grated fresh ginger

3 tablespoons Ceylon curry powder (page 17)

1–2 teaspoons chilli powder

2 teaspoons salt

1 tablespoon vinegar

5 cm (2 in) cinnamon stick

4 cardamom pods

250 ml (8½ fl oz/1 cup) thick coconut milk (pages 8–9)

Cut the pork into cubes. Soak the tamarind pulp in 125 ml (½ cup) hot water for 10 minutes. Squeeze to dissolve the pulp in the water, then strain, discarding the seeds and fibre. Set aside.

Heat the oil in a large saucepan over low heat. Add the curry leaves and fenugreek seeds, if using, and cook until they start to brown. Add the onion and garlic and cook until the onion turns golden. Increase the heat to high and add the ginger, curry powder, chilli powder, salt, vinegar and pork, stirring thoroughly until the meat is well coated. Add the tamarind liquid, cinnamon stick and cardamom pods, cover, and continue cooking over low heat until the pork is tender, about 1 hour. Add the coconut milk and cook, uncovered, for a further 10 minutes.

Pour the sauce into a separate saucepan and set aside. Return the pork to the pan and allow to cook in its own fat – you may need to add 1 tablespoon oil extra if it isn't fatty enough. When the pork is nicely brown, return the sauce to the pan and cook, uncovered, until the sauce has thickened. Serve hot with rice.

Lampries Curry

Serves: 16–18

500 g (1 lb 2 oz) blade (chuck) steak

500 g (1 lb 2 oz) diced leg of lamb or mutton

5 teaspoons salt, plus extra to taste

8 cardamom pods

20 whole black peppercorns

500 g (1 lb 2 oz) chicken thighs

500 g (1 lb 2 oz) pork belly, diced

20 g (¾ oz) ghee

2 tablespoons oil

4 onions, finely chopped

8 garlic cloves, finely chopped

1 tablespoon finely chopped fresh ginger

2 teaspoons curry leaves, crushed

¼ teaspoon fenugreek seeds (optional)

4 tablespoons Ceylon curry powder (page 17)

1 teaspoon ground turmeric

2 teaspoons chilli powder

1 cinnamon stick

1 teaspoon ground cardamom

3 pandanus leaves

2 stems lemongrass, bruised, or 4 strips
lemon zest

2 tablespoons lemon juice

625 ml (21 fl oz/2½ cups) thin coconut milk
(pages 8–9)

625 ml (21 fl oz/2½ cups) thick coconut
milk (pages 8–9)

Put the steak and mutton in a large saucepan with enough cold water to cover. Add 2 teaspoons of the salt, the cardamom pods and peppercorns. Cover and simmer for 30 minutes, then add the chicken and simmer for 15 minutes. Allow to cool, then strain and cut all the meats into very small dice, discarding the bones.

Heat the ghee and oil in a large saucepan over medium heat. Add the onion, garlic, ginger and curry leaves and cook until the onion is golden. Add the fenugreek seeds, if using, and cook for 1 minute, then add the curry powder, turmeric, chilli powder, cinnamon stick, ground cardamom, pandanus leaves, lemongrass, remaining salt, lemon juice, diced pork and half of each of the coconut milks. Stir well, cover, and cook over low heat for 30 minutes. Return the meats to the pan, add the remaining coconut milk and simmer, uncovered, for 1½ hours, or until the meat is tender and sauce has thickened. Serve hot.

Note

The meat in this curry is diced twice, before and after cooking. This allows each compact serve to include a mixture of all the meats.

Vegetables

🔥

Karavadu Vambotu Curry
Salt fish and eggplant curry

Serves: 6

250 g (9 oz) dried salted fish (glossary)

500 g (1 lb 2 oz) eggplants (aubergines)

1 teaspoon ground turmeric

1 teaspoon salt

125 ml (4 fl oz/½ cup) oil for frying

12 large banana chillies, deseeded and split lengthways

10 garlic cloves, peeled and left whole

1 large onion, thinly sliced

1 tablespoon tamarind pulp

60 ml (2 fl oz/¼ cup) malt vinegar

750 ml (25½ fl oz/3 cups) coconut milk (pages 8–9)

3 tablespoons Ceylon curry powder (page 17)

1 cinnamon stick

½ teaspoon salt, or to taste

1–2 teaspoons sugar, to taste

Rinse the dried fish, drain well, then cut into 5 cm (2 in) pieces. Slice the eggplants thickly, rub each slice with the turmeric and salt and set aside in a colander for 30 minutes. Drain the liquid given off from the eggplant slices and dry each slice on paper towel.

Heat half the oil in a frying pan over medium heat. Separately fry the dried fish, chillies, garlic, onion and eggplant, removing each to a plate once cooked – it may be necessary to replenish the oil as it is used up, as the eggplant absorbs quite a lot.

Soak the tamarind pulp in the vinegar for 10 minutes. Squeeze to dissolve the pulp in the vinegar, then strain, discarding the seeds and fibre.

Put the coconut milk into a saucepan with the curry powder, cinnamon stick, tamarind liquid and salt. Stir until the mixture comes to the boil, then add the cooked fish, chilli, garlic, onion and eggplant and keep stirring frequently as the mixture cooks. When it is thick, add the sugar and stir to dissolve before serving.

Elolu Kiri Hodhi
Vegetable curry

Serves: 4–6

This classic white curry is very versatile and you can use any of your favourite vegetables.

750 ml (25½ fl oz/3 cups) thin coconut milk
(pages 8–9)

1 onion, thinly sliced

2 fresh green chillies, deseeded and split
lengthways

½ teaspoon ground turmeric

2 garlic cloves, thinly sliced

½ teaspoon finely grated fresh ginger

5 cm (2 in) cinnamon stick

1 pandanus leaf

1 stem lemongrass, bruised, or 2 strips
lemon zest

8 curry leaves

750 g (1 lb 11 oz) mixed sliced vegetables

salt, to taste

250 ml (8½ fl oz/1 cup) thick coconut milk
(pages 8–9)

Put all the ingredients, except the sliced vegetables, salt and thick coconut milk, into a large saucepan and simmer gently, uncovered, for about 10 minutes. Add the sliced vegetables and salt and cook gently until the vegetables are just tender. Add the thick coconut milk and simmer for about 5 minutes. Serve with rice, other curries and accompaniments.

Cadju Curry
Cashew curry

Serves: 4–6

A curry of fresh cashew nuts is one of the delights of Sinhalese cooking. Fresh cashew nuts are not obtainable except in the country in which they are grown, but raw cashew nuts, from health food shops and Asian grocery stores, make a very good substitute if soaked overnight in cold water.

Proceed as for vegetable curry (above), but use 250 g (9 oz/1⅔ cups) raw cashew nuts instead of the sliced vegetables. Simmer for about 30 minutes, or until the cashew nuts are tender. Serve with rice and other accompaniments.

Bandakka Curry
Okra curry

Serves: 4

....

250 g (9 oz) tender okra

½ teaspoon ground turmeric

oil for deep-frying

1 small onion, finely chopped

2 fresh green chillies, deseeded and sliced

6 curry leaves

1 teaspoon ground coriander, dry-roasted

½ teaspoon ground cumin, dry-roasted

1 teaspoon pounded Maldive fish (smoked dried tuna) or dried prawn (shrimp) powder

5 cm (2 in) cinnamon stick

½ teaspoon salt

¼ teaspoon chilli powder (optional)

375 ml (12½ fl oz/1½ cups) coconut milk (pages 8–9)

Rinse the okra, drain, then trim off the tops and slice in half lengthways. Rub with the ground turmeric to coat.

Heat the oil in a large heavy-based saucepan over medium heat. When the oil is hot, deep-fry the okra until lightly browned. Drain on paper towel.

Put all the remaining ingredients into a saucepan over low heat and simmer for about 10 minutes, or until the onion is cooked. Add the fried okra, simmer until tender and remove from the heat. Serve with rice.

Rabu Kolle Mallung
Shredded radish leaf

Serves: 4

green leaves from 1 bunch small red
  radishes, rinsed

1 onion, finely chopped

½ teaspoon ground turmeric

2 teaspoons Maldive fish (smoked dried
  tuna) or dried prawn (shrimp) powder

1 tablespoon lemon juice

½ teaspoon salt

½ teaspoon chilli powder

2 tablespoons desiccated (shredded)
  coconut

Finely chop the radish leaves and put them into a saucepan with all the remaining ingredients, except the coconut. Cover and cook over medium heat, or until all the moisture has almost evaporated. Add the coconut and stir over low heat until the coconut absorbs all the liquid – a mallung must be fairly dry in consistency. Serve with rice and curries.

Gova Mallung
Shredded cabbage

Serves: 6

250 g (9 oz) cabbage, finely shredded

1 onion, finely chopped

2 fresh green chillies, deseeded and
  chopped

¼ teaspoon ground turmeric

¼ teaspoon freshly ground black pepper

½ teaspoon ground black mustard seeds

1 teaspoon salt

2 teaspoons pounded Maldive fish
  (smoked dried tuna) or dried prawn
  (shrimp) powder

45 g (1½ oz/½ cup) desiccated (shredded) or
  freshly grated coconut

Rinse the cabbage, then drain well and put it into a large saucepan with all the remaining ingredients, except the coconut. Cover and cook over medium heat until the cabbage is tender, stirring from time to time. Uncover, then add the coconut and toss over low heat until the coconut absorbs the liquid. Serve hot or cold.

Sapattu Mal Curry
Hibiscus curry

Serves: 6

The single red hibiscus is used in sambols, curries and as a refreshing drink – it is said to have the effect of purifying the blood.

12 single red hibiscus flowers (*Hibiscus rosa sinensis*)

150 g (5½ oz/1 cup) plain (all-purpose) flour

a pinch of salt

1 egg, beaten

oil for frying

Curry

1 tablespoon oil

1 small onion, finely chopped

2 fresh green chillies, deseeded and sliced

¼ teaspoon ground turmeric

2 teaspoons pounded Maldive fish (smoked dried tuna) or dried prawn (shrimp) powder

1 cinnamon stick

500 ml (17 fl oz/2 cups) thin coconut milk (pages 8–9)

125 ml (4 fl oz/½ cup) thick coconut milk (pages 8–9)

2 teaspoons vinegar or lemon juice

Wash the flowers, shake off all the water or blot with paper towel. Pick off the calyx and the stamen. Sift the flour and salt together and add the egg and just enough water to make a smooth batter.

Heat the oil in a large heavy-based saucepan over medium heat. Dip each flower first in the batter, shaking off any excess, then gently lower into the hot oil and deep-fry until golden. Drain on paper towel and set aside.

To make the curry, heat the oil in a saucepan over low heat. Add the onion and chilli and cook until golden brown. Add the turmeric and stir for 1 minute, then add the Maldive fish, cinnamon stick and thin coconut milk; season with salt, to taste. Bring to the boil, then reduce the heat to low and add the hibiscus flowers. Simmer over low heat for 5 minutes, then add the thick coconut milk and simmer for a further 5 minutes. Remove from the heat and stir in the vinegar; serve hot.

Mallung
Shredded green leaves with coconut

Serves: 6

A 'mallung' is very much part of the Sri Lankan diet. It can be best described as a very tasty dry accompaniment to be eaten with rice. One or two different mallungs are served with every meal and play an important part in nutrition because this is how the people of Sri Lanka get their vitamins. The leaves of many common plants are used; some of them grown in Western countries too, such as the yellow flowered cassia. The flowers are dried to make an infusion for medicinal purposes, and the leaves are stripped from the stems and used for mallung – they have a pleasant sour flavour. Tender passionfruit leaves also make a delicious mallung. One of the most popular mallungs is made with *gotukolle*, the medicinal herb gotu kola. It resembles violet leaves, but is a type of cress which grows near water. As a substitute, use flat-leaf (Italian) parsley.

130 g (4½ oz/2 cups) finely shredded green leaves

1 onion, finely chopped

2 fresh green chillies, deseeded and chopped (optional)

½ teaspoon ground turmeric

2 teaspoons pounded Maldive fish (smoked dried tuna) or dried prawn (shrimp) powder

2 tablespoons lemon juice

1 teaspoon salt

2–3 tablespoons freshly grated or desiccated (shredded) coconut

Rinse the green leaves and place them into a saucepan with all the remaining ingredients, except the coconut. If there is not much water clinging to the leaves after washing, add a sprinkling of water. Stir well, cover, and cook over medium heat for about 6 minutes. Uncover, then add the coconut and toss over low heat until the coconut absorbs all the liquid. Remove from the heat and serve hot or cold as an accompaniment to rice.

Vatakka Curry
Yellow pumpkin curry

Serves: 6

500 g (1 lb 2 oz) pumpkin (winter squash), peeled, deseeded and cut into large chunks

1 small onion, finely chopped

2 garlic cloves, finely chopped

3 fresh green chillies, deseeded and chopped

8–10 curry leaves

½ teaspoon fenugreek seeds

½ teaspoon ground turmeric

2 teaspoons pounded Maldive fish (smoked dried tuna) or dried prawn (shrimp) powder

375 ml (12½ fl oz/1½ cups) thin coconut milk (pages 8–9)

1 teaspoon salt

125 ml (4 fl oz/½ cup) thick coconut milk (pages 8–9)

1 teaspoon black mustard seeds

Place the pumpkin in a large saucepan with all the ingredients, except the thick coconut milk and mustard seeds. Bring slowly to simmering point and cook until the pumpkin is just tender.

Meanwhile, grind the mustard seeds using a mortar and pestle and stir into the thick coconut milk. Add to the pumpkin and cook for a further 5 minutes, or until tender. Serve hot.

Alu Kehel Curry
Green banana curry

Serves: 6

The green bananas used for this curry must be really unripe, otherwise the texture will not be suitable for this dish.

4–5 very green, hard unripe bananas

1 teaspoon salt

1 teaspoon ground turmeric

60 ml (2 fl oz/¼ cup) oil, plus extra for handling

500 ml (17 fl oz/2 cups) coconut milk (pages 8–9)

1 small onion, thinly sliced

2 fresh green chillies, deseeded and sliced

2 teaspoons pounded Maldive fish (smoked dried tuna) or dried prawn (shrimp) powder

¼ teaspoon fenugreek seeds

8 curry leaves

1 cinnamon stick

Rub your hands with oil or wear disposable kitchen gloves before starting to handle unripe bananas, as this prevents staining. Peel the bananas, cut them in halves widthways and then into slices or quarters lengthways. Rub with the salt and turmeric.

Heat the oil in a small frying pan over medium heat. Add the banana pieces, in batches, and cook for 3–4 minutes, or until they are golden brown all over. Set aside.

Put all the remaining ingredients into a separate saucepan and simmer until the onion is soft. Add the fried banana and simmer until the sauce has thickened. Serve hot.

Vatakolu Curry
Ridged gourd curry

Serves: 6

These ridged gourds (luffa) have a very sweet and delicate flavour and are sometimes sold at farmers' markets or in Asian grocery stores. They are generally around 45 cm (18 in) long, tapered at one end with very clearly delineated straight ridges along their length. They should not be confused with the lumpy-ridged, shiny-skinned bitter melon (gourd).

500 g (1 lb 2 oz) ridged gourd (luffa)

2 tablespoons oil

8 curry leaves

1 onion, thinly sliced

2 fresh green chillies, deseeded and sliced

1 teaspoon ground coriander

½ teaspoon ground cumin

¼ teaspoon ground turmeric

¼ teaspoon ground chilli powder (optional)

375 ml (12½ fl oz/1½ cups) coconut milk (pages 8–9)

1 teaspoon salt

Peel the gourd – a potato peeler is useful for removing the sharp ridges – and cut into slices widthways.

Heat the oil in a saucepan over medium heat and cook the curry leaves, onion and chilli until the onions are golden. Add the ground spices and stir for a few seconds, then add the gourd and cook for 10 minutes, stirring regularly. Add the coconut milk and salt and bring to the boil, stirring occasionally, then reduce the heat to low and simmer until the gourd is tender. Don't cover the pan, as this might cause the coconut milk to curdle.

Leeks Mirisata
Leeks fried with chilli

Serves: 6

60 ml (2 fl oz/¼ cup) oil

4 leeks, white part only, rinsed and
thinly sliced

½ teaspoon ground turmeric

1 teaspoon chilli powder, or to taste

2 tablespoons pounded Maldive fish
(smoked dried tuna)

1 teaspoon salt

Heat the oil in a large saucepan over low heat. Add the leek and cook for 5 minutes, then stir in the remaining ingredients, cover, and cook for 30 minutes, stirring occasionally, until the leek has reduced in volume. Uncover and cook until the liquid has evaporated. Serve with a rice meal and other curries.

Paripoo
Lentils, Sri Lankan-style

Serves: 6

500 g (1 lb 2 oz/2 cups) red lentils

500 ml (17 fl oz/2 cups) thin coconut milk (pages 8–9)

1 dried red chilli, chopped

2 teaspoons pounded Maldive fish (smoked dried tuna) or dried prawn (shrimp) powder

1 teaspoon ground turmeric

1 tablespoon ghee or oil

6 curry leaves

2 onions, thinly sliced

20 cm (8 in) piece pandanus leaf

1 cinnamon stick

1 stem lemongrass or 1 strip lemon zest

125 ml (4 fl oz/½ cup) thick coconut milk (pages 8–9)

Wash the lentils well, removing any that float to the surface, then drain. Place in a saucepan with the thin coconut milk, chilli, Maldive fish and turmeric. Bring to the boil, then reduce the heat to low, cover, and simmer until the lentils are just tender.

Heat the ghee in a separate saucepan over low heat. Add the curry leaves, onion, pandanus leaf, cinnamon stick and lemongrass and cook until the onion is brown. Remove half of the onion to a plate to use as a garnish. Add the remaining onion to the lentil mixture, along with the thick coconut milk, and stir to combine. Season with salt, to taste, and simmer until the lentils are very soft and the consistency of runny porridge. Serve with rice and curries.

Accompaniments

Frikkadels
Dutch forcemeat balls

Makes: about 40

20 g (¾ oz) butter

1 small onion, finely chopped

500 g (1 lb 2 oz) minced (ground) beef

40 g (1½ oz/½ cup) fresh breadcrumbs

1½ teaspoons salt

½ teaspoon freshly ground black pepper

2 tablespoons chopped fresh dill

½ teaspoon ground cinnamon

¼ teaspoon ground cloves

1 garlic clove, crushed

1 teaspoon finely grated fresh ginger

2 teaspoons Worcestershire sauce or
 lemon juice

1 egg, beaten

dry breadcrumbs for coating

oil or ghee for deep-frying

Heat the butter in a small frying pan over low heat. Add the onion and cook until it is soft. Cool slightly and place in a bowl along with the minced beef, breadcrumbs, salt, pepper, dill, cinnamon, cloves, garlic, ginger and Worcestershire sauce. Use your hands to combine thoroughly.

Shape the mince mixture into small balls with a 2.5 cm (1 in) diameter. Put the egg in one bowl and the dry breadcrumbs in a shallow dish. Dip each meatball first into the egg and then roll in the dry breadcrumbs to coat, shaking off any excess.

Heat the oil in a deep-fryer or large heavy-based frying pan and deep-fry the balls until golden brown. Drain on paper towel before serving as an accompaniment.

Bombili Mirisata
Bombay duck chilli fry

Serves: 4

125 ml (4 fl oz/½ cup) oil

6 Bombay duck (glossary), cut into 5 cm
  (2 in) lengths

2 onions, thinly sliced

2 garlic cloves, finely chopped

3 dried red chillies, deseeded and chopped

lemon juice, to taste

Heat the oil in a small saucepan and cook the Bombay duck until crisp. Drain on paper towel.

Pour off half the oil from the pan and cook the onion and garlic until golden. Add the chilli and cook for 2–3 minutes, then return the Bombay duck to the pan and stir-fry for 1 minute. Add the lemon juice and salt to taste. Serve hot or at room temperature.

Ogu Ruloung
Scrambled eggs with flavourings

Serves: 6

This is part of the traditional range of stringhopper accompaniments. If stringhoppers aren't available, try it with the mock Stringhopper pilau (page 21).

8 large eggs

2 tablespoons finely chopped fresh dill

1 teaspoon salt

½ teaspoon freshly ground black pepper

2 tablespoons ghee or oil

6 spring onions (scallions), thinly sliced

1 teaspoon dried curry leaves, crushed, or
   1 tablespoon fresh curry leaves, chopped

Beat the eggs lightly with 2 tablespoons water. Stir in the dill, salt and pepper.

Heat the ghee in a frying pan over medium heat. Add the spring onion and cook until pale golden, then add the curry leaves and cook for a further 1 minute. Add the egg and cook over low heat, stirring, until the egg begins to set – do not cook until dry; the eggs should be moist and creamy.

Thambung Hodhi
Sour soup

Serves: 4

2 tablespoons ground coriander

1 tablespoon ground cumin

1 dried red chilli (optional)

½ teaspoon whole black peppercorns

8 curry leaves

1 tablespoon tamarind pulp

1 onion, thinly sliced

4 garlic cloves, peeled and left whole

Dry-fry the coriander, cumin, chilli, if using, peppercorns and curry leaves in a saucepan over medium heat, shaking the pan or stirring constantly, until the spices are aromatic. Add 1.25 litres (42 fl oz/5 cups) hot water, the tamarind, onion and garlic and bring to the boil. Reduce the heat to low and simmer for 20 minutes, or until the onion and garlic are soft. Serve in small bowls for sipping between mouthfuls of rice.

Prawn Blacan

Serves: 18–20

This is an essential accompaniment to Lampries (page 26), the festive meal wrapped in banana leaves.

250 g (9 oz/1 cup) dried prawn (shrimp) powder

45 g (1½ oz/½ cup) desiccated (shredded) coconut

2 teaspoons chilli powder, or to taste

2 onions, chopped

5 garlic cloves, sliced

1 tablespoon finely chopped fresh ginger

170 ml (5½ fl oz/⅔ cup) lemon juice

1 teaspoon salt, or to taste

Heat the prawn powder in a dry frying pan over low heat for a few minutes, stirring. Remove to a plate. Put the desiccated coconut in the same pan and heat, stirring, until a rich chestnut brown colour. Remove to a plate. Put the remaining ingredients into a food processor and process until smooth. Add the prawn powder and coconut and process to combine, adding a little water if needed to bind the ingredients. Place in a plate and shape into a round, flat cake. Serve with rice and curries.

Abba
Country mustard

Makes: about 1 cup

This mustard should be made with tiny black or brown mustard seeds. It is used in Sri Lanka for serving as an accompaniment to meats, for spreading on sandwiches, or for adding to certain stews or curries. Left-over turkey is made into a rich stew and a good spoonful of this mustard is added, with perhaps some chilli thrown in for good measure, and it is then very aptly called 'turkey devil'! It is amazingly similar to the French mustard sold in pots.

80 g (2¾ oz/½ cup) black mustard seeds

white, malt or red wine vinegar

1 garlic clove (optional)

1 tablespoon finely chopped fresh ginger

2 teaspoons sugar

Put the mustard seeds into a glass or earthenware bowl and pour over just enough vinegar to cover. Let stand for 15 minutes.

Put the mustard seeds and vinegar into a food processor with the garlic, if using, and ginger and process until the seeds are pulverised. Add the sugar and some salt to taste. Store in a sterilised airtight jar. Kept in the refrigerator the mustard will keep for many months.

Abba Achcharu
Mustard pickle

80 g (2¾ oz/½ cup) black mustard seeds

750 ml (25½ fl oz/3 cups) white or malt vinegar

2 teaspoons salt

1 teaspoon ground turmeric

250 g (9 oz) red Asian shallots, peeled

12 fresh red or green chillies

185 g (6½ oz/1 cup) sliced unripe papaya (optional)

125 g (4½ oz/1 cup) sliced green beans

125 g (4½ oz/1 cup) cauliflower florets

100 g (3½ oz) carrots, cut into thin matchsticks

1 bitter melon (gourd), deseeded and cut into strips

6 garlic cloves

1 tablespoon finely grated fresh ginger

3 teaspoons sugar

Put the mustard seeds in a bowl with just enough of the vinegar to cover and leave to soak overnight.

Put the remaining vinegar in a saucepan with the salt, turmeric and shallots and bring to the boil for 1 minute. Lift out the shallots with a slotted spoon, leave to drain and cool. Repeat with the chilli, papaya, beans, cauliflower and carrot – allowing extra time for the beans, cauliflower and carrot, which should be tender but still crisp to bite. Reserve the cooking vinegar. When all the vegetables are drained and cooled, put them into a sterilised airtight jar.

Put the mustard seeds and soaking liquid into a food processor with all the remaining ingredients and the reserved cooking vinegar and process to combine. Pour over the vegetables in the jar, adding more vinegar to cover the vegetables if needed. If the jar has a metal lid, cover with 2 layers of baking paper before sealing. This mustard pickle will keep for many months. To avoid spoiling, always use a clean dry spoon.

Kiri Hodhi
Coconut milk gravy

Serves: 6

Serve as an accompaniment to be spooned over rice or sipped between mouthfuls of rice and curry. If a less rich result is required, substitute low-fat milk or water for part of the coconut milk.

1 tablespoon fenugreek seeds

1 large onion, finely chopped

12 curry leaves

1 cinnamon stick

2 fresh green chillies, deseeded and split lengthways

¼ teaspoon ground turmeric

1 teaspoon salt

2 teaspoons pounded Maldive fish (smoked dried fish) or dried prawn (shrimp) powder

625 ml (21 fl oz/2½ cups) thin coconut milk (pages 8–9)

500 ml (17 fl oz/2 cups) thick coconut milk (pages 8–9)

lemon juice, to taste

Wash the fenugreek seeds and soak in cold water for at least 30 minutes.

Put the fenugreek seeds into a saucepan with all the remaining ingredients, except the thick coconut milk and lemon juice. Simmer over low heat until the onion has reduced to a pulp and the milk has been thickened by the fenugreek seeds. Stir well, then add the thick coconut milk and heat without boiling. Stir in the lemon juice and add more salt, if needed. Serve hot in small bowls.

Note

If a thicker soup is preferred, add a few slices of potato to the ingredients in the pan before simmering.

Vambotu Pahi
Eggplant pickle

2 teaspoons salt, plus extra to taste

2 teaspoons ground turmeric

2 large eggplants (aubergines), cut into 1 cm (½ in) thick slices

oil for frying

1 tablespoon black mustard seeds

125 ml (4 fl oz/½ cup) vinegar

1 onion, finely chopped

4 garlic cloves, sliced

1 tablespoon finely chopped fresh ginger

1 tablespoon ground coriander

2 teaspoons ground cumin

1 teaspoon ground fennel

125 g (4½ oz/½ cup) tamarind pulp

3 fresh green chillies, deseeded and sliced

8 cm (3¼ in) cinnamon stick

1 teaspoon chilli powder (optional)

2 teaspoons sugar

Rub the salt and turmeric over the eggplant slices and drain in a colander for at least 1 hour. Dry with paper towel.

Heat about 2.5 cm (1 in) of the oil in a large heavy-based frying pan. Add the eggplant and cook until brown on both sides. Remove to a plate, reserving 125 ml (4 fl oz/½ cup) of the oil in the pan.

Put the mustard seeds and vinegar in a food processor and process to a pulp. Add the onion, garlic and ginger, and process to make a smooth paste. Set aside.

Dry-fry the coriander, cumin and fennel in a small frying pan over low heat, shaking the pan or stirring, until toasted.

Soak the tamarind pulp in 190 ml (6½ fl oz/¾ cup) hot water for 10 minutes. Squeeze to dissolve the pulp in the water, then strain, discarding the seeds and fibre.

Heat the reserved oil and cook the mustard mixture for 5 minutes. Add the roasted spices, chilli, cinnamon stick, tamarind liquid and chilli powder, if using. Add the eggplant and any oil, cover, and simmer for 15 minutes. Remove from the heat, stir in the sugar and add salt to taste. Cool and store in sterilised airtight jars. The eggplant pickle will keep for many months. To avoid spoiling, always use a clean dry spoon.

Thora Malu Moju
Fish pickle

Serves: 8–10

500 g (1 lb 2 oz) fish steaks, such as
    Spanish mackerel, cut into slices

salt

ground turmeric

250 ml (8½ fl oz/1 cup) oil

1 tablespoon finely chopped garlic

1 tablespoon finely chopped fresh ginger

2 teaspoons black mustard seeds

250 ml (8½ fl oz/1 cup) vinegar

10 curry leaves

2 tablespoons ground coriander

1 tablespoon ground cumin

½ teaspoon fenugreek seeds

1 teaspoon ground fennel (optional)

1 pandanus leaf (optional)

2 teaspoons chilli powder

1 teaspoon ground turmeric

1 tablespoon sugar

1 teaspoon salt

Wipe the fish clean with damp paper towel and rub each steak with the salt and turmeric. Heat 125 ml (4 fl oz/½ cup) of the oil in a frying pan over low heat. Add the fish and cook until brown and crisp. Set aside on a plate.

Put the garlic, ginger, mustard seeds and 125 ml (4 fl oz/ ½ cup) of the vinegar in a food processor and process to a smooth purée.

Heat the remaining oil in a saucepan over low heat. Add the curry leaves, coriander, cumin, fenugreek seeds, fennel and pandanus leaf, if using, and cook, stirring until the spices are dark brown but do not allow them to burn. Add the chilli powder and turmeric and cook for a few seconds longer, then add the mustard mixture and stir-fry for a further 3 minutes. Add the remaining vinegar with the sugar and salt, bring to the boil, then add the fish. Reduce the heat to low and simmer for 30 minutes. Remove from the heat and cool. Store in sterilised airtight jars for up to 1 month.

To serve, heat 2 tablespoons of ghee or oil and fry the required amount of the fish pickle to heat through.

Thora Malu Siyambala Achcharu
Seer fish pickle with tamarind

Serves: 10–12

The popular seer fish of Sri Lanka and India is also known as Spanish mackerel or king mackerel. Any firm, dark-fleshed fish will be suitable.

500 g (1 lb 2 oz) fish steaks, such as
  Spanish mackerel

1 teaspoon salt

½ teaspoon ground turmeric

60 ml (2 fl oz/¼ cup) oil

125 g (4½ oz/½ cup) tamarind pulp

190 ml (6½ fl oz/¾ cup) vinegar

3 tablespoons ground coriander

1½ tablespoons ground cumin

3 teaspoons ground fennel

1 tablespoon chilli powder

sugar, to taste

Wipe the fish clean with damp paper towel. Cut the fish into large pieces and rub over with the salt and turmeric. Heat the oil in a frying pan over low heat. Add the fish and cook until brown and crisp. Drain off the oil, leaving the fish in the pan, and set aside.

Soak the tamarind pulp in the vinegar for 10 minutes. Squeeze to dissolve the pulp in the vinegar, then strain, discarding the seeds and fibre.

Dry-fry the coriander, cumin and fennel separately in a frying pan over low heat, until aromatic and the colour darkens slightly. Remove to a plate when roasted.

Combine the tamarind liquid, roasted spices and chilli powder in a bowl. Return the fish in the pan to the heat and pour the spices over the fish, simmering for a few minutes. Add some salt and sugar, to taste. Remove from the heat and cool. Store in sterilised airtight jars for up to 1 month. Serve as an accompaniment with rice and curries.

Dehi Achcharu
Pickled lemons or limes

thin-skinned lemons or limes

coarse salt

malt vinegar

Put the whole fruits in a saucepan with enough water to cover and bring to the boil for 10 minutes, or until each lemon splits slightly. Remove from the heat, drain, and when cool enough to handle, stuff 1 tablespoon of salt into the split in each lemon, pressing it in well. Arrange the lemons in a sterilised wide-mouthed jar, pour over the vinegar to cover, seal tightly and leave for 6 months before using. The lemons will keep indefinitely and are an ingredient in Beef smoore (page 58) and Lime and date chutney (page 94).

Dehi Lunu
Salted limes or lemons

At my grandmother's house there were always large stoneware jars of salted limes, steeped so long that the fruit were a translucent brown and the juice around them turned to clear amber jelly. When limes or lemons are in season it is a good idea to put down a couple of bottles of this salt-preserved fruit. They will keep indefinitely, and can be made into chutneys, pickles or simple curry accompaniments.

25–30 thin-skinned limes or lemons

rock salt

Wash and dry the fruit. Starting at the end opposite the stem, cut each lime into quarters up to, but not through, the stem. Open the slits slightly and stuff each with about 1 tablespoon of salt. Put each into sterilised airtight jars as it is done – if possible use stone jars, or glass jars with plastic, not metal, lids. Cover tightly and leave in the sun every day for 3 weeks, then store in the cupboard for 6 months, or longer.

Dehi Achcharu Temperado
Lime oil pickle

Makes: 2 cups

8 Salted limes or lemons (opposite)

6 fresh red chillies

6 fresh green chillies

2 tablespoons black mustard seeds

1 tablespoon cumin seeds

2 teaspoons fennel seeds

2 teaspoons black cumin seeds

2 teaspoons fenugreek seeds

125 ml (4 fl oz/½ cup) mustard oil or peanut oil

2 tablespoons sesame oil

6 garlic cloves, thinly sliced

1 tablespoon finely grated fresh ginger

½ teaspoon asafoetida powder

1 stem lemongrass, bruised, or 2 strips lemon zest

1 cinnamon stick

125 ml (4 fl oz/½ cup) vinegar

1 teaspoon chilli powder

Separate the limes into quarters and cut each quarter into 3 or 4 pieces. Remove the stems and seeds of the chillies and cut into halves or quarters, depending on their size.

In a dry frying pan, roast the mustard, cumin, fennel, black cumin and fenugreek seeds separately over medium heat, stirring constantly to prevent burning. When they smell aromatic, remove to a plate to cool.

Heat the mustard oil and sesame oil in a large heavy-based frying pan over low heat. Add the garlic and ginger and cook until golden, then add the remaining ingredients, bring to the boil, reduce the heat to low and simmer for 10 minutes, stirring constantly. Remove from the heat, discard the cinnamon stick and lemongrass and allow to cool. Store in sterilised airtight jars for many months. To avoid spoiling, always use a clean dry spoon.

Dehi Rata Indi Chutney
Lime and date chutney

20 large dried red chillies, stalks and seeds removed, chopped

1 tablespoon black mustard seeds

500 ml (17 fl oz/2 cups) malt vinegar

20 garlic cloves, peeled

2 tablespoons finely grated fresh ginger

660 g (1 lb 7 oz/3 cups) white sugar

500 g (1 lb 2 oz) dried dates, halved and stones removed

6–8 salted or pickled limes or lemons (page 92), thinly sliced

125 g (4½ oz/1 cup) sultanas (golden raisins)

Put the chilli in a bowl with the mustard seeds and vinegar and leave to soak overnight.

Put the chilli and mustard seeds, along with the vinegar, into a food processor. Add the garlic and ginger and process until smooth.

Put the chilli mixture and sugar into a large saucepan and bring to the boil. Reduce the heat to low and simmer until the sauce thickens. Add the dates, lime and sultanas and bring back to the boil, then reduce the heat to low and simmer for 15–20 minutes. Pour into sterilised airtight jars. Will keep for 6 months or longer.

Sambols

Pipinja Sambola
Cucumber sambol

Makes: 2 cups

1 large or 2 small green cucumbers, peeled
  and thinly sliced

1 teaspoon salt

125 ml (4 fl oz/½ cup) thick coconut milk
  (pages 8–9)

1 fresh red chilli, deseeded and sliced

1 fresh green chilli, deseeded and sliced

1 small red onion, thinly sliced

2 tablespoons lemon juice

Put the cucumber in a bowl, sprinkle with the salt and let stand for at least 30 minutes. Press out all the liquid and if too salty, rinse with cold water. Drain well. Mix with the remaining ingredients and serve as an accompaniment to a curry meal.

Dehi Lunu Sambola
Salted lime sambol

Makes: 4 cups

1 salted or pickled lime or lemon (page 92)

2 tablespoons finely sliced red Asian shallot
  or onion

2 fresh red or green chillies, deseeded
  and sliced

Cut the lime or lemon into small pieces and mix with the shallots and chillies in a small bowl. Serve with a rice and curry meal. A teaspoon of this is sufficient for a serving, as it is meant to be only a taste accent.

Kalupol Sambola
Roasted coconut sambol

Makes: 2 cups

In Sri Lanka this is made with fresh coconut, roasted in the ashes of the fire until dark brown, then ground on a large stone, but this version is a lot easier to make.

90 g (3 oz/1 cup) desiccated (shredded) coconut

2 onions, finely chopped

1 teaspoon salt

2 teaspoons Maldive fish (smoked dried tuna) or dried prawn (shrimp) powder

60 ml (2 fl oz/¼ cup) lemon juice

Dry-fry the coconut in a heavy-based frying pan over low heat and stir constantly until it is a fairly deep chestnut brown, but be careful not to burn it. Spread onto a large plate to cool.

Combine all the ingredients in a food processor and process to a smooth paste – it may be necessary to add a little more onion or lemon juice if the mixture is too dry.

Shape the sambol into a round flat cake and mark the top in a criss-cross pattern with a fork or the back of a knife. Serve with rice and curry.

Badhapu Lunu Sambola
Fried onion sambol

Makes: 1–2 cups

125 ml (4 fl oz/½ cup) oil

2 large onions, thinly sliced

6 dried red chillies, deseeded and broken into pieces

2 tablespoons Maldive fish (smoked dried tuna) or dried prawn (shrimp) powder

2 teaspoons salt, or to taste

2 tablespoons lemon juice

Heat the oil in a frying pan over low heat. Add the onion and cook until it is soft. Add the chilli and Maldive fish, cover, and cook for 10–15 minutes, stirring occasionally, until the oil separates. Add the salt and lemon juice and cook for a further 3–4 minutes. Serve with rice and curries.

Koonee Sambola
Shrimp sambol

The dried shrimp, or *koonee*, used in this delicious sambol are very small – no thicker than a piece of twine. They are sold in Asian grocery stores.

1 small onion, finely chopped

3 fresh red chillies, deseeded and finely chopped

1 teaspoon fenugreek seeds

1 tablespoon lemon juice

1½ teaspoons salt

½ teaspoon ground turmeric

3 tablespoons dried shrimp

135 g (5 oz/1½ cups) freshly grated or desiccated (shredded) coconut

Put all the ingredients, except the coconut, into a saucepan. Add 125 ml (4 fl oz/½ cup) water, cover, and simmer over low heat until the onion is soft. Add the coconut and toss, uncovered, until the coconut absorbs all the liquid. Taste and add extra salt and lemon juice if necessary. Serve with rice and curries.

Pol Sambola
Coconut sambol

Makes: 1–2 cups

90 g (3 oz/1 cup) desiccated (shredded) coconut

1 teaspoon salt

1 teaspoon chilli powder, or to taste

2 teaspoons paprika

2 teaspoons Maldive fish (smoked dried tuna) or dried prawn (shrimp) powder (optional)

2 tablespoons lemon juice, or to taste

1 red onion, finely chopped

2–3 tablespoons hot milk

Combine the coconut, salt, chilli powder, paprika and Maldive fish, if using, in a bowl. Add the lemon juice, onion and milk and use your hands to mix everything together so that the coconut is evenly moistened. Pile into a small serving bowl.

Note

You can add 1–2 deseeded and finely chopped fresh red or green chillies for a hotter version.

Lunu Miris Sambola
Ground onion and chilli sambol

Makes: 2 cups

This simple sambol is as basic to the food of Sri Lanka as salt and pepper to Western food. Very hot, very acid and distinctly salty, it is often the only accompaniment served with rice, boiled yams or sweet potato, or any of the starches that are staples of the native diet.

10 dried red chillies

1 tablespoon pounded Maldive fish (smoked dried tuna) or dried shrimp

1 small onion, chopped

lemon juice and salt, to taste

Remove the stalks from the chillies and, if a less hot result is preferred, shake out the seeds. Pound all the ingredients together using a mortar and pestle. It may be pulverised in a blender, but a wet result is not desirable – it should be more like a paste. Serve with rice or Pittu (page 27).

Karavila Sambola
Bitter melon sambol

Serves: 4–6

3 bitter melons (gourds)

½ teaspoon ground turmeric

½ teaspoon salt

oil for frying

1 brown onion, thinly sliced

2 fresh green chillies, deseeded and sliced

lemon juice, to taste

Wash the bitter melons and cut widthways into thin slices. Rub with the turmeric and salt.

Heat the oil in a large heavy-based saucepan over low heat. Add the melons and cook until golden brown on both sides. Drain on paper towel, then combine in a bowl with the onion and chillies. Season with lemon juice and more salt, if needed.

Seeni Sambola
Chilli sambol

Makes: 2 cups

Chilli sambol is a popular accompaniment to rice and curry. Thanks to convenient tinned 'prawns (shrimp) in spices' (sold in Asian grocery stores), this simple chilli sambol can be prepared in a fraction of the time it takes to make the original and tastes just as good. Add more chilli powder if you prefer a hotter flavour.

125 ml (4 fl oz/½ cup) oil

4 onions, thinly sliced

2 teaspoons chilli powder, or to taste

170 g (6 oz) tinned prawns (shrimp) in spices

2 tablespoons vinegar

salt, to taste

2 teaspoons sugar

Heat the oil in a large frying pan over low heat. Add the onion and cook until soft. It is important to cook the onion slowly; the liquid in the onion must evaporate if the sambol is to keep well. When the onion is golden brown, add the chilli powder, prawns in spices and vinegar. Stir thoroughly, cover, and simmer for 10 minutes. Uncover the pan and continue simmering, stirring occasionally, until the liquid evaporates and the oil starts to separate. Season with salt, to taste. Remove from the heat, stir in the sugar and allow to cool. Spoon into a sterilised airtight jar and keep for up to 1 month. Use in small quantities.

Badhapu Vambotu Sambola
Fried eggplant sambol

....

2 teaspoons salt

2 teaspoons ground turmeric

2 eggplants (aubergines), cut into 1 cm
(½ in) thick slices

oil for frying

3 fresh red or green chillies, deseeded and
chopped

2 small onions, thinly sliced

60 ml (2 fl oz/¼ cup) thick coconut milk
(pages 8–9)

lemon juice, to taste

Rub the salt and turmeric over the eggplant and drain in a colander for at least 1 hour. Dry with paper towel.

Heat about 2.5 cm (1 in) of the oil in a large heavy-based frying pan over low heat. Add the eggplant and cook until brown on both sides. Cool and place in a bowl with the chilli, onion and coconut milk, then add a squeeze of lemon juice to taste.

Moong Ata Sambola
Bean sprout sambol

....

90 g (3 oz/1 cup) fresh bean sprouts

3 fresh green chillies, deseeded and sliced

1 small onion, thinly sliced

1 tablespoon grated fresh coconut or
desiccated (shredded) coconut

1 teaspoon salt

1 tablespoon lemon juice, or to taste

Wash the bean sprouts thoroughly and drain well. Mix all the ingredients together in a bowl and serve with rice and curries.

Cakes
and
Sweets

🔥

Thala Guli
Sesame seed and palm sugar balls

Makes: 20 balls

One of Sri Lanka's best-known local sweetmeats, these are also sold on the road to Kandy, the ancient hill capital and favourite tourist resort, by villagers who also offer young coconuts for drinking.

155 g (5½ oz/1 cup) sesame seeds

250 g (9 oz) grated dark palm sugar (jaggery)

a generous pinch of salt

1 teaspoon sesame oil (optional)

Grind the sesame seeds in a spice grinder until fine and powdery, or pound using a mortar and pestle, a little at a time, until the seeds are crushed and oily. As each batch is done, turn into a bowl.

Add the palm sugar and salt and use your hands to mix well – the heat of your hands and vigorous kneading will help to soften the palm sugar, and after a while the mixture will hold together. If this is taking too long, add the sesame oil until the mixture just holds its shape.

Take 1 teaspoon of the mixture at a time and roll into neat balls. These may be arranged on a serving plate but traditionally they are wrapped in rectangular pieces of baking paper that have been fringed at the ends. The paper is twisted on either side of the balls so each one looks like a miniature Christmas cracker. Serve at the end of a curry meal, or as a between-meal treat.

Bolo De Coco
Coconut cake

Makes: one 25 cm (10 in) square cake

In Sri Lanka, the moist, rich flesh of coconut fresh from the tree is grated, then ground finely on a stone slab. The resulting texture is much like finely ground almonds, but wetter. If you live in a country where fresh coconuts are available, use two medium-sized nuts. If, however, you can only obtain the desiccated (shredded) variety, treat it in the way described below and you will still have a delicious coconut cake.

270 g (9½ oz/3 cups) desiccated (shredded) coconut

4 eggs, separated

440 g (15½ oz/2 cups) sugar, plus 55 g (2 oz/¼ cup) extra

350 g (12½ oz/2 cups) rice flour

150 g (5½ oz/1 cup) self-raising flour

2 teaspoons baking powder

½ teaspoon ground cardamom

¼ teaspoon ground cloves

¼ teaspoon ground cinnamon

1 tablespoon rosewater

125 g (4½ oz) raw cashew nuts or blanched almonds, finely chopped

Preheat the oven to 160°C (320°F). Line a 25 cm (10 in) square cake tin with baking paper and grease the paper with melted butter.

Put 135 g (5 oz/1½ cups) of the desiccated coconut and 375 ml (12½ fl oz/1½ cups) water into a food processor and process until the coconut is finely ground. Repeat with the remaining coconut and another 375 ml (12½ fl oz/1½ cups) water.

Beat the eggs yolks, sugar and 2 tablespoons of the coconut mixture in the bowl of an electric mixer until light and creamy. Add the remaining coconut and beat well. Sift the combined flours, baking powder and ground spices into the mixture, then add the rosewater and cashew nuts and mix well.

In a separate bowl, beat the egg whites until stiff peaks form, add the extra sugar and beat again until thick and glossy. Fold into the coconut mixture until just combined. Pour into the prepared tin and bake for 1¼–1½ hours, or until risen and golden brown on top. A fine skewer inserted in the centre of the cake should come out clean. Half cool the cake in the tin, then turn out and cool completely on a wire rack. Cut into squares to serve.

Bolo Folhado
Many-layered cake

Serves: about 20

Curiously like a large, rich Danish pastry, this is one of the most popular sweets handed down from the time the Portuguese ruled Sri Lanka. It is not made among the Sinhalese, but is very much prized by the descendants of the Dutch and Portuguese, the Burghers. Only a thin layer of filling is necessary between the layers of pastry.

Pastry

450 g (1 lb/3 cups) plain (all-purpose) flour

a pinch of salt

125 g (4½ oz) butter

1 teaspoon fresh compressed yeast or
   ½ teaspoon dried yeast

190 ml (6½ fl oz/¾ cup) lukewarm milk

1 teaspoon sugar

2 egg yolks

1 egg, beaten

Filling

440 g (15½ oz/2 cups) sugar

390 g (14 oz/2½ cups) raw cashew nuts, finely chopped

1 tablespoon rosewater, or to taste

To make the pastry, sift the flour and salt into a mixing bowl. Add one-quarter of the butter and use your fingertips to rub into the flour until the mixture resembles breadcrumbs. Make a well in the centre.

Dissolve the yeast in 60 ml (2 fl oz/¼ cup) water, then add the milk, sugar and beaten egg yolks. Add to the flour, stirring well to make a soft dough. Turn out onto a lightly floured work surface and knead lightly until it is free from cracks – add a little more flour if it is too soft. Wrap in plastic wrap and refrigerate for 30 minutes.

Roll out the dough to make a 60 × 20 cm (24 × 8 in) rectangle and spread two-thirds of the surface with the remaining butter, leaving a border at the edges. Fold the unbuttered third to the centre and fold the last third over it. Turn the dough so the folds are to the right and left of you, then press with a rolling pin to seal the open ends and roll out again. Fold into thirds as before, wrap in plastic wrap and chill. Repeat the rolling and folding twice more. Chill the dough until firm between each rolling to keep the layers of butter from melting out.

Divide the dough into 4 equal portions, one just slightly larger than the other three. Roll out the smaller portions to make 3 circles with a 28 cm (11 in) diameter, then roll the larger one to make a circle with a 30 cm (12 in) diameter. Line a baking tray or flan (tart) tin with baking paper and put the largest circle of pastry on it. Re-roll any left-over pastry to make shapes to use for decoration.

To make the filling, put the sugar and 250 ml (8½ fl oz/1 cup) water into a large heavy-based saucepan and bring to the boil. Boil for 5 minutes, or until a heavy syrup forms. Reduce the heat, stir in the cashew nuts and simmer until the mixture thickens but is not stiff. Cool slightly, stir in the rosewater, then allow to cool completely.

Preheat the oven to 200°C (400°F). Spread one-third of the filling over the first circle of pastry, leaving a 2.5 cm (1 in) border around the edge. Cover with a second circle of pastry and spread with another one-third of the filling as before. Place the third pastry circle on top and spread over the remaining filling, then top with the final pastry circle. Brush the border of the bottom layer with beaten egg, then fold it over the upper layers and flute around the edge, or press with a fork to seal. Decorate the top with the pastry trimmings. Brush over with the remaining egg and bake in the oven for 15 minutes, then reduce the heat to 170°C (340°F) and bake for a further 35–40 minutes or until browned. Remove from the heat and cool, then cut into thin wedges to serve.

Breudher

Makes: 2 large cakes

Originally a Dutch recipe, this rich yeast cake is traditionally served at Christmas and New Year.

310 g (11 oz) unsalted butter

310 g (11 oz/1⅓ cups) caster (superfine) sugar

1 quantity Basic dough (page 30)

5 eggs

2 teaspoons natural vanilla extract

250 g (9 oz/2 cups) sultanas (golden raisins)

Cream the butter and sugar in the bowl of an electric mixer until light and fluffy. Add the dough in small pieces, beating well, until all the dough has been incorporated.

Add the eggs, one at a time, beating well after each addition. Stir in the vanilla and sultanas until well combined.

Lightly grease two 2.5 litre (85 fl oz/10 cup) kugelhopf or bundt tins. Divide the dough between the tins and leave in a warm, draught-free place for 30 minutes, or until almost doubled in size.

Preheat the oven to 160°C (320°F). Bake the breudher for 30–35 minutes, or until well risen and golden brown on top. If the top starts to brown too soon, cover with foil and cook until a thin skewer inserted into the centre of the loaf comes out clean. Remove from the oven and cool in the tins for 10 minutes, then turn out onto a wire rack to cool completely. Serve the bread sliced, spread with unsalted butter and sprinkled with caster sugar or, if preferred, with thin slices of Dutch Edam cheese.

Avocado Fool

Serves: 4–6

Before I came to Australia, believe it or not, I had never tried avocados in any other way than as a dessert. They grew plentifully in the tropical country I had lived in for most of my life, and when they were in season we indulged in the smooth, green fruit mashed with sweetened condensed milk. (Because there was no dairy industry in Sri Lanka, fresh cream was out of reach.) I looked up the only cookbook we used in Sri Lanka, *The Ceylon Daily News Cookbook*, and sure enough, the recipe was for a dessert. No wonder I was stuck in a rut of thinking of avocados as a sweet. I have now learned to appreciate them in salads, but I could not overlook the way I had enjoyed them for many years, and this is why avocado fool is the only recipe for avocados in this book. I did modify it by using sugar and cream instead of sweetened condensed milk but, if truth be told, I do still enjoy it with condensed milk.

3 large ripe avocados

caster (superfine) sugar, to taste

250 ml (8½ fl oz/1 cup) pouring
  (single/light) cream

a dash of rum (optional)

Cut the avocados in half lengthways, remove the stones and reserve. Scoop the flesh from the shells into a bowl and mash smoothly with a fork. Add sugar to taste, then stir in the cream and rum, if using. Place into a serving bowl, return the stones to the pulp (to stop the avocado from discolouring), then cover with plastic wrap, making sure it lies directly on the surface of the fruit, and refrigerate until chilled, about 3 hours.

Note

Extra whipped or sweetened cream may be piped over the top of the dessert and a few thin slices of avocado (sliced at the last moment) used for decoration.

Foguete
Deep-fried pastry with sweet filling

Makes: 24

This is one of the Portuguese recipes left by the one-time conquerors of Sri Lanka. The translation of foguete is 'rocket', because they look like miniature fireworks. Little hollow tubes of pastry are fried, cooled and filled with a sweet mixture. Very often they are dipped in a crystallising syrup to coat the pastry, which keeps them crisp for a few days, but also makes the overall effect very sweet. I prefer to fill them just before they are to be served and omit the crystallising process.

Metal cannoli moulds are ideal for rolling the foguete, but otherwise use twelve 8 cm (3¼ in) lengths of wooden dowelling with a 2 cm (¾ in) diameter – you will need to grease them with butter before rolling the pastry over.

Pastry

300 g (10½ oz/2 cups) plain (all-purpose) flour

a pinch of salt

60 g (2 oz) butter

2 eggs

2 egg yolks (egg whites reserved separately)

1 tablespoon icing (confectioners') sugar, plus extra for dusting

1 teaspoon natural vanilla extract

oil for frying

Fillings

Avocado fool (page 109) (see note)

pineapple or melon jam

155 g (5½ oz/1 cup) chopped raw cashew nuts mixed with 125 g (4½ oz/1 cup) chopped raisins

1 quantity Bolo folhado filling (page 106)

Note

Follow the instructions for making the Avocado fool on page 109, but whip the cream and avocado after mashing with the sugar before piping into the pastry shells.

To make the pastry, sift the flour and salt into a mixing bowl. Use your fingertips to rub the butter into the flour until it resembles fine breadcrumbs. Make a well in the centre.

In a separate bowl, beat together the eggs and egg yolks, add the icing sugar and vanilla extract and 2 tablespoons of cold water – if the eggs are very large, the water may not be necessary. Add to the flour and mix well to make a firm pastry. Turn out onto a lightly floured work surface and knead for 10 minutes, or until the pastry is smooth and shiny. Wrap in plastic wrap and refrigerate for 1 hour.

Divide the pastry into portions. Roll each portion out on a lightly floured work surface, as thinly as possible. Cut into lengths a little narrower than the cannoli moulds, about 6 cm (2½ in), and long enough to fit loosely around the moulds. Wet a thin strip at one end of each length with egg white and pinch both ends together around the mould to give a fluted effect. If the pastry is too loose, pinch it together on the opposite side to the join, making 2 fluted ridges, but don't make it too tight a fit or it will be difficult to slip off the mould later.

Heat a little oil in a large heavy-based saucepan over medium heat. When the oil is hot, drop in the tubes, a few at a time, and cook until pale golden. Remove from the oil and when cool enough to handle, gently slip the mould from the centre, return the tubes to the oil and continue cooking until golden brown. Drain on paper towel and cool completely. If not using immediately, the tubes can be stored in an airtight container for up to 3 days.

Just before you are ready to serve, use a teaspoon or piping bag to fill the tubes with the filling of your choice, depending on its consistency. Dust with icing sugar and serve.

Traditional Christmas Cake

Makes: one 25 cm (10 in) cake

Many people have told me that after making this recipe they never use any other for a fruitcake. It is rich, dark and moist, fragrant with spice and laden with fruit. The semolina and ground nuts make its texture quite different from a cake made with flour.

240 g (8½ oz/1½ cups) raisins, chopped

375 g (13 oz/3 cups) sultanas (golden raisins), chopped

250 g (9 oz) mixed glacé fruit, such as pineapple, apricot and quince, chopped (avoid using figs)

250 g (9 oz) chopped preserved ginger

500 g (1 lb 2 oz) chow chow preserves (glossary) (see note)

125 g (4½ oz/⅔ cup) mixed peel, chopped

250 g (9 oz) glacé cherries, halved

250 g (9 oz/1⅔ cups) raw cashew nuts or blanched almonds, finely chopped

60 ml (2 fl oz/¼ cup) brandy

375 g (13 oz) butter

500 g (1 lb 2 oz) caster (superfine) sugar

12 egg yolks (reserve 6 egg whites for this recipe)

2 teaspoons finely grated lemon zest

1½ teaspoons ground cardamom

1 teaspoon ground cinnamon

1 teaspoon freshly grated nutmeg

¾ teaspoon ground cloves

2 tablespoons natural vanilla extract

1 tablespoon natural almond extract

2 tablespoons rosewater, or to taste

1 tablespoon honey

250 g (9 oz/2 cups) fine semolina

6 egg whites

1 quantity Almond paste (page 114) for icing (optional)

Note

Chow chow preserves can be purchased at Asian grocery stores. If unavailable, substitute melon and ginger jam or ginger marmalade.

Variation

For a gluten-free version, omit the semolina and use a fine cornmeal, sold as 'dusting polenta'.

Line a 25 cm (10 in) round or square cake tin with 3 layers of brown paper, then one layer of baking paper liberally brushed with melted butter. To insulate the tin even more, wrap the outside with a sheet of newspaper folded into 3 and secure it with kitchen string.

Combine the raisins, sultanas, mixed glacé fruit, preserved ginger, chow chow preserves, mixed peel, glacé cherries and cashew nuts in a large bowl. Pour over the brandy, cover, and set aside. (This step can be done the day before, allowing the fruit more time to soak in the brandy, if desired.)

Preheat the oven to 130°C (265°F). Cream together the butter and sugar until light and fluffy. Add the egg yolks, one at a time, beating well after each addition. Add the lemon zest, spices, vanilla and almond extracts, rosewater and honey and mix well. Add the semolina and beat until well combined.

Transfer the mixture to a large bowl or pan and use your hands to mix in the fruit until thoroughly combined – it's much easier than a spoon and professional pastry cooks do it this way.

In a separate bowl, beat the egg whites until stiff peaks form, then fold through the fruit mixture until just combined. Pour into the prepared cake tin and bake in the oven for 2¼–2½ hours, covering the cake with foil after the first hour to prevent over-browning. The cake will be very rich and moist when done. If you prefer a darker and drier result, bake for 4½– 5 hours – it will not be dry, but certainly firmer than if you cook for a shorter time. Allow to cool completely, preferably overnight, then remove the paper and wrap the cake in foil. A tablespoon or two of brandy may be sprinkled over the cake just before wrapping. If desired, ice the cake with the almond paste. This cake can be stored in an airtight container for 1 year or longer.

Almond Paste

255 g (9 oz/2½ cups) ground almonds

500 g (1 lb 2 oz/4 cups) icing (confectioners') sugar, sifted

1 small egg, beaten

1 tablespoon brandy

1 tablespoon sherry

½ teaspoon natural almond extract (optional)

1 egg white, beaten, for brushing

Mix together the ground almonds and icing sugar in a large bowl, add the combined egg, brandy, sherry and almond extract, if using, then knead until the mixture holds together. Roll out half the almond paste on a work surface dusted with icing sugar and cut to fit the top of the cake. Brush the Traditional Christmas cake (page 112) with egg white, then place the almond paste on top and press lightly with a rolling pin. Roll the remaining almond paste into a strip to fit around the side of the cake.

Alla Aluwa
Potato halva

Makes: about 18 pieces

After a rich curry meal, serve this sweetmeat with black coffee.

330 g (11½ oz/1½ cups) sugar

375 ml (12½ fl oz/1½ cups) milk

410 g (14½ oz) tinned sweetened condensed milk

125 g (4½ oz) ghee or butter

230 g (8 oz/1 cup) mashed potato

2 tablespoons rosewater

155 g (5½ oz/1 cup) cashew nuts, finely chopped (optional)

1 teaspoon ground cardamom (optional)

Put the sugar, milk, condensed milk and ghee into a large heavy-based saucepan over medium heat. Stir constantly, until the mixture reaches soft-ball stage, or 116°C (240°F) on a sugar thermometer. (Alternatively, to test for soft-ball stage, drop a little of the mixture into a cup of ice-cold water. If it firms enough to be moulded into a soft ball, it has reached the required temperature.)

Remove from the heat, add the mashed potato and beat well until very smooth. Return to the heat and cook to soft-ball stage once more. Remove from the heat, stir in the rosewater, cashew nuts and cardamom, if using, and mix well.

Pour into a well-buttered shallow dish or baking tin. Press lightly with a piece of buttered banana leaf or foil to smooth and flatten the surface. Allow to cool and set, then cut into diamond shapes or squares to serve.

Love Cake (1)

Serves: 25

125 g (4½ oz) butter, softened

250 g (9 oz/2 cups) coarse semolina

10 egg yolks

500 g (1 lb 2 oz) caster (superfine) sugar

360 g (12½ oz/2⅓ cups) raw cashew nuts, finely chopped

2 tablespoons rosewater

1 tablespoon honey

1 teaspoon freshly grated nutmeg

1 teaspoon finely grated lemon zest

1 teaspoon ground cinnamon

Preheat the oven to 160°C (320°F). Lightly grease a 20 cm (8 in) square cake tin and line with 2 layers of baking paper.

Mix together the butter and semolina until combined.

In a separate bowl, beat the egg yolks and sugar until thick and creamy. Add the semolina mixture and beat until well combined. Add the remaining ingredients and mix thoroughly. Pour into the prepared tin and bake for about 50–60 minutes, or until the top is nicely browned and the cake is cooked through.

Love Cake (2)

Serves: 25

A very popular cake in Sri Lanka, though no one knows why it is called by this name. There are many recipes – some use butter while others do not; some insist that only egg yolks should be used and others include egg whites as well. This is my favourite version.

7 eggs, separated

500 g (1 lb 2 oz) caster (superfine) sugar

250 g (9 oz/2 cups) coarse semolina

360 g (12½ oz/2⅓ cups) raw cashew nuts, finely chopped

2 tablespoons rosewater

2 tablespoons honey

½ teaspoon finely grated lemon zest

½ teaspoon ground mace or freshly grated nutmeg

½ teaspoon ground cardamom

½ teaspoon natural almond extract (optional)

Preheat the oven to 150°C (300°F). Lightly grease a 20 cm (8 in) square cake tin and line with 2 layers of baking paper. Brush the paper with melted butter.

Beat together the egg yolks and caster sugar until light and creamy. Stir in the semolina, cashew nuts, rosewater, honey, lemon zest, spices and almond extract, if using.

Beat the egg whites in a separate bowl until stiff peaks form. Fold into the cake batter, then pour into the prepared tin. Bake for about 1 hour, or until the cake is golden on top and feels firm to the touch. If the cake starts to brown too quickly, cover the top with foil. Remove from the oven and leave in the tin to cool before cutting. Do not attempt to turn out this cake – instead, cut into small squares and lift each one separately onto a serving plate.

Vattalappam
Spicy coconut custard

Serves: 6–8

This rich custard, Malaysian in origin, is very popular in Sri Lanka. If dark palm sugar (jaggery) is not available, substitute with 115 g (4 oz/½ cup) firmly packed dark brown sugar and 125 ml (4 fl oz/½ cup) maple syrup.

Coconut milk

180 g (6½ oz/2 cups) desiccated (shredded) coconut

625 ml (21 fl oz/2½ cups) milk

180 g (6½ oz/1 cup) finely chopped dark palm sugar (jaggery)

4 eggs, lightly beaten (they should not be frothy)

190 ml (6½ fl oz/¾ cup) evaporated milk

½ teaspoon ground cardamom

¼ teaspoon ground mace

a pinch of ground cloves

1 tablespoon rosewater

To make the coconut milk, put the coconut and milk in a saucepan and bring to the boil, then remove from the heat and cool slightly. Knead firmly with your hands for a few minutes and strain through a fine sieve, squeezing out as much liquid as possible. Set aside.

Preheat the oven to 170°C (340°F). Put the palm sugar and 125 ml (4 fl oz/½ cup) water in a saucepan over low heat and stir to dissolve the sugar. Allow to cool slightly, then add to the egg and stir to combine. (If you are using dark brown sugar and maple syrup, add them directly to the beaten eggs.) Add the coconut milk and stir well to combine. Strain through a fine sieve into a large pitcher, then add the evaporated milk, spices and rosewater.

Pour into six or eight 125 ml (4 fl oz/½ cup) capacity ramekins or moulds. Place the ramekins in a deep baking dish and pour in enough water to come halfway up the sides of the ramekins. Bake in the oven for 1¼ hours, or until set. Remove from the oven and allow to cool, then refrigerate for at least 6 hours, and serve chilled.

The Philippines

A mixture of Malay, Chinese and Spanish — with just a touch of American influence — is the combination that makes the food of the Philippines and the people themselves the exotic blend of East and West that they are.

Originally the Philippine islands were inhabited by Negritos, an ethnic group in the Malayo-Polynesian region. Then came traders from Malaya, Indonesia and China who settled and intermarried. In the sixteenth century came the Spanish conquerors, who stayed for 400 years. The Spanish made a lasting impact on the way of life in the Philippines. They brought Catholicism, which was wholeheartedly embraced by the Filipinos, making the Philippines the only Christian country in Asia. They also introduced many of their foods and special festive dishes, so that now the cuisine of the Philippines is as much influenced by Spanish tastes as it is by the Malay and Chinese way of cooking.

In the Philippines, as in the rest of Asia, rice is the staple food of the people. Rice and fish make up the native breakfast, but more popular is a breakfast of spicy native sausages, called *longaniza*, made of pork and flavoured with pepper, garlic and other ingredients and briefly cured. These are fried and kept warm while left-over cooked rice is fried in the pork fat that remains. Fried eggs are also popular at breakfast. Sometimes Continental types of bread, such as *pan de sal*, are served in place of rice. Hot chocolate and *ensaimadas* is a favourite mid-morning snack. *Ensaimadas* are made from a dough like that used for brioche, rich with butter, sugar and eggs; the unusual feature is that they have a filling and sometimes a topping of finely grated mature cheese, but the sweet, savoury combination is delicious (see recipe, page 159). Lunch and dinner are both big meals in the Philippines, and may include four or five courses – soup, fish, meat, fresh fruit and finally a rich, sweet dessert. This is eating Spanish-style. If the meal is served Filipino-style, then everything is put on the table at once.

Between lunch and dinner there is yet another meal, *merienda*, which can best be compared to an English high tea. It consists not only of sandwiches and cakes, but also lumpia (a type of spring roll), a dish of *pancit* (fried noodles with vegetables, prawns/shrimp, pork, chicken or ham), and at least a couple of local sweets made from grated coconut, coconut milk, glutinous rice, sweet potato or tropical fruits.

In spite of the Spanish influence, many truly native dishes are very popular. Adobo is the most popular and best known dish of the Philippines. It is a method of cooking, not one precise and unalterable recipe, and thus you may find chicken adobo, pork adobo, or a combination of both. It is typical of the flavours Filipinos find pleasing – vinegar, garlic and pepper. Sometimes coconut milk is one of the ingredients, sometimes not. It is this combination of flavours that helps tenderise the meat and give it flavour – the meat is pre-soaked in the vinegar mixture for an hour or more before cooking.

If annatto seeds, which are used as a colouring agent in many Filipino dishes, are not available, a similar effect can be achieved by using ¼ teaspoon of paprika and ⅛ teaspoon of ground turmeric to replace 1 teaspoon annatto seeds. The resulting colour should be bright orange. Be careful not to cook the paprika and turmeric mixture on its own or it may burn – add it instead with the onion and garlic. Similarly, palm vinegar, which is typically used for cooking in the Philippines, is much milder than wine vinegar, but this can be used if diluted with water.

Serving and eating a Filipino meal

Tables often have a raised circular turntable on which the dishes of food are placed to make it easy to present the food to everyone sitting at the table without having to pass dishes to and fro. Flat dinner plates, spoons, knives and forks are used, with bowls for soup. The old custom of eating with the fingers is mainly retained in villages. Wine is seldom served with a meal – water being the popular drink, as in most Asian countries. However, the food of the Philippines is more suited to being served with wine than are the hot spicy foods of neighbouring countries. Coffee is the preferred hot beverage among Filipinos.

Utensils

The traditional way of cooking rice in the Philippines is to wash it several times, then cook it in earthenware pots lined with banana leaves to prevent it from sticking to the base of the pot. In the Philippines the rounded pan, shaped like a wok, is called a *carajay* (pronounced 'cara-hai') and most likely was introduced by the Chinese. It is useful for stir-fried noodle dishes, but these days it is no problem to use the modern equipment of a Western kitchen.

Your Filipino Shelf

annatto seeds	misu (roughly mashed salted soy beans)
bay leaves	olive oil
black pepper, whole and freshly ground	paprika
breadcrumbs, fresh and dried	saffron strands
cellophane (bean thread) noodles	shiitake mushrooms, dried
chickpeas (garbanzo beans), dried	shrimp sauce
coconut milk and cream (pages 8–9)	soy sauce, light and dark
coconut, desiccated (shredded)	Spanish saffron
cornflour (cornstarch)	spring roll wrappers
fish sauce	tamarind pulp
ground rice	turmeric, ground
lard	vinegar

Seafood

Pesa
Fish with ginger

Serves: 4

2 × 500 g (1 lb 2 oz) whole flathead or other delicate white fish

60 ml (2 fl oz/¼ cup) oil

3 tablespoons finely chopped fresh ginger

1 teaspoon freshly ground black pepper

rice water (see note)

½ teaspoon salt

4 spring onions (scallions), 2 whole, 2 chopped

1 coriander (cilantro) sprig

Misu tomato sauce

2 tablespoons chopped pork fat

2 garlic cloves, crushed

1 onion, finely chopped

2 tomatoes, peeled and chopped

2 tablespoons misu (mashed salted soy beans) or yellow miso

1 tablespoon vinegar

¼ teaspoon freshly ground black pepper

Clean and scale the fish, leaving the head on. Wipe inside the fish cavity with damp paper towel that has first been dipped in coarse salt. Trim any long spines or fins neatly. Set aside.

To make the sauce, heat the pork fat in a saucepan over low heat. Add the garlic and onion and cook until soft. Add the tomato and cook to a pulp, then add the vinegar and pepper, stirring well, and simmer to heat through. Keep warm.

Heat the oil in a wok or large heavy-based frying pan over low heat. Add the ginger and cook until soft and golden. Add the pepper, then place the fish in the pan and add just enough rice water to almost cover. Add the salt, lay a spring onion over each fish, cover, and simmer for 8 minutes, or until the fish is cooked. Carefully transfer the fish to a serving dish, scatter over the chopped spring onion and garnish with coriander. Pour the cooking liquid around the fish and serve the misu tomato sauce and some white rice on the side.

Note

'Rice water' is the water in which rice has been washed prior to cooking.

Ukoy
Prawn and sweet potato fritters

Makes: about 20

1½ teaspoons salt

250 g (9 oz) raw small school prawns (shrimp)

150 g (5½ oz/1 cup) plain (all-purpose) flour

80 g (2¾ oz/½ cup) ground rice

30 g (1 oz/¼ cup) cornflour (cornstarch)

2 eggs

½ teaspoon freshly ground black pepper

125 g (4½ oz/1 cup) peeled and grated sweet potato

90 g (3 oz/1 cup) fresh bean sprouts, trimmed and blanched

4 spring onions (scallions), thinly sliced

oil for deep-frying

Note

Make a garlic and vinegar dipping sauce by crushing 1 garlic clove with 1 teaspoon salt and adding to 60 ml (2 fl oz/¼ cup) mild vinegar. Serve with the fritters.

Put 250 ml (8½ fl oz/1 cup) water into a large saucepan with the salt and bring to the boil. Gently lower in the prawns and when the water returns to the boil, cover, and cook for 3–4 minutes, or until the prawns turn pink. Drain the prawns, reserving the cooking liquid. Remove the heads – in the Philippines the prawns are left in their shells and this may be done if they are very small. If they are not, the shells are somewhat tough and I prefer to peel them, leaving only the tails on.

Put the flour, ground rice and cornflour into a large bowl. Beat the eggs and add the pepper and 250 ml (8½ fl oz/1 cup) of the prawn cooking liquid, making up the measure with water if needed. Add to the dry ingredients and beat well to make a smooth batter.

Add the sweet potato, bean sprouts and half of the spring onion to the batter, stirring well to combine.

Heat the oil in a wok or large heavy-based frying pan over medium heat. Take 1 tablespoon of the batter at a time, placing 2 or 3 prawns and a sprinkling of spring onion on top of the spoon before sliding it into the hot oil. Spoon the oil over them as they cook and when the underside is golden brown, turn and fry the other side. The oil should not be too hot or they will darken before they are cooked and crisp. Drain on paper towel and serve hot.

Guinataan Hipon
Prawns in coconut milk

Serves: 6

750 g (1 lb 11 oz) raw prawns (shrimp)

500 ml (17 fl oz/2 cups) thick coconut milk
(pages 8–9)

1 tablespoon finely chopped garlic

1 teaspoon finely chopped fresh ginger

1 teaspoon salt

¼ teaspoon freshly ground black pepper

Rinse and drain the prawns but do not peel them. Put them into a saucepan with the coconut milk, garlic, ginger, salt and pepper and bring to the boil, stirring to combine. Reduce the heat to low and simmer for 15 minutes, stirring frequently, until the prawns turn pink. Serve with hot white rice.

Cardillo
Fried fish with tomatoes and egg

Serves: 4

500 g (1 lb 2 oz) skinless, boneless,
firm white fish fillets

2 tablespoons lard or olive oil

1 garlic clove, crushed

1 onion, thinly sliced

2 tomatoes, thinly sliced

2 eggs, lightly beaten

Cut the fish into strips. Rub a little salt over the fish to coat.

Heat 1 tablespoon of the lard in a wok or large heavy-based frying pan over medium heat. Add the fish and stir-fry, in batches, until golden brown. Remove to a plate once cooked.

Heat the remaining lard over low heat. Add the garlic and cook until golden, then add the onion and tomato and season with salt, to taste. Cook until the tomato is soft and pulpy, then add 125 ml (4 fl oz/½ cup) water and simmer for 3–5 minutes. Return the fish to the wok, then remove from the heat and add the egg, stirring to combine and heat through until the egg is set. Serve hot.

Kilaw
Marinated fish salad

Serves: 8

Fish is marinated in lime or lemon juice, the acid turning the fish white and opaque so that it looks 'cooked', although the texture is a little different. I have used this recipe with many kinds of fish and found that the best results were with snapper (porgy), redfish and flathead, but any delicately flavoured white fish is suitable.

1 kg (2 lb 3 oz) skinless, boneless, firm white fish fillets, such as flathead, snapper (porgy) and redfish

250 ml (8½ fl oz/1 cup) lemon juice

1 teaspoon salt, plus extra to taste

2 onions, very thinly sliced

250 ml (8½ fl oz/1 cup) coconut cream (pages 8–9)

1 garlic clove, crushed

1 teaspoon finely grated fresh ginger

½ teaspoon freshly ground black pepper

¼ teaspoon ground turmeric

1 large red capsicum (bell pepper), deseeded and diced

1 large green capsicum (bell pepper), deseeded and diced

6 spring onions (scallions), thinly sliced

3–4 firm red tomatoes, peeled and diced

1 large lettuce, leaves separated

Cut the fish into bite-sized pieces and place in a non-metallic bowl with the lemon juice, tossing to cover the fish. Add the salt and onion and stir with a wooden spoon. Do not use metal utensils. Cover and refrigerate for at least 8 hours, stirring once or twice while marinating.

In a large bowl, combine the coconut cream, garlic, ginger, pepper and turmeric and mix well to combine.

Drain the fish, discarding the lemon juice. Add the coconut dressing, capsicums, spring onion and tomato and toss together to coat the fish and vegetables in the dressing. Serve the mixture in a dish lined with lettuce leaves.

Arroz a la Paella
Rice with chicken and seafood

Serves: 6–8

Among the many dishes with Spanish flavour found in the Philippines is this favourite rice dish popular for feast days.

1 × 1.5 kg (3 lb 5 oz) whole chicken

500 g (1 lb 2 oz) pork chops (cutlets)

1 raw lobster tail (optional)

2 hot chorizo (Spanish sausages)

olive oil for frying

500 g (1 lb 2 oz) raw prawns (shrimp), peeled and deveined, tails left intact

500 g (1 lb 2 oz) fresh mussels, scrubbed and beards removed

Sofrito

½ teaspoon saffron strands

2 tablespoons boiling water

60 ml (2 fl oz/¼ cup) olive oil

2 large onions, finely chopped

5 garlic cloves, finely chopped

250 g (9 oz/1 cup) tinned chopped tomatoes

3 teaspoons salt

3 teaspoons paprika

500 g (1 lb 2 oz/2½ cups) long-grain rice

1.1 litres (37 fl oz/4½ cups) hot chicken or fish stock

155 g (5½ oz/1 cup) peas

1 red capsicum (bell pepper), deseeded and thinly sliced

Joint the chicken (see page 12), cut it into serving pieces and season well with salt and freshly ground black pepper.

Cut the pork chops into dice, discarding the bones. Chop the lobster tail, if using, into large slices, including the shell. Pierce the chorizos in a few places with a sharp knife, then place into a saucepan with enough water to cover and bring to the boil. Reduce the heat to low and simmer for 5 minutes. Drain well and slice into rounds. Set aside.

In a large heavy-based frying pan, heat enough olive oil to cover the base of the pan. Add the chicken and cook on all sides over medium heat, until golden. Remove to a plate. Add the lobster and cook for 1–2 minutes, or until the shell turns pink. Remove to a plate. Add the chorizo to the pan and cook for 5 minutes, then remove to a plate and drain on paper towel. Add the pork to the pan and cook for 10 minutes, then remove to a plate. Discard the oil in the pan.

To make the sofrito, combine the saffron strands and boiling water in a bowl and leave to soak. Heat the olive oil in a large heavy-based saucepan over medium heat. Add the onion and cook until soft and golden. Add the garlic, the soaked saffron and the soaking liquid and the tomatoes and cook until the tomatoes are soft and pulpy. Add the salt and paprika and stir well, then add the rice to the pan and stir over medium heat for 3–4 minutes to coat. Add the hot stock, stir well and bring to the boil. Add the chicken, pork, chorizo and lobster, then reduce the heat to low, cover, and simmer for 15 minutes. Add the prawns and mussels, pushing the mussels into the rice so they will cook in the steam. Do not use any mussels that are not tightly closed before cooking, and discard any mussels that do not open during cooking. Do not stir. Scatter the peas over the top, cover, and cook for a further 15 minutes, or until the rice is cooked through and most of the liquid has been absorbed. Garnish with the capsicum to serve.

Meat

Empanadas
Meat–filled pastries

Makes: about 24

Filling

3 rashers (slices) bacon, diced

1 tablespoon lard or oil

2 garlic cloves, finely chopped

1 onion, finely chopped

250 g (9 oz) minced (ground) pork and veal, or chorizo sausage, finely chopped

125 g (4½ oz) finely chopped raw chicken

¾ teaspoon salt

½ teaspoon freshly ground black pepper

2 tablespoons tomato sauce (ketchup)

3 hard-boiled eggs, chopped

2 tablespoons chopped pickled gherkins (dill pickles)

Pastry

300 g (10½ oz/2 cups) plain (all-purpose) flour

½ teaspoon salt

1 tablespoon sugar

1 egg, separated, both yolk and white lightly beaten

60 ml (2 fl oz/¼ cup) melted butter or margarine

lard or oil for deep-frying

To make the filling, cook the bacon in a small frying pan over low heat until it is cooked through. Remove to a plate.

Heat the lard in the same pan over low heat. Add the garlic and onion and cook until soft and golden. Increase the heat, add the meats and fry until they start to change colour. Add the salt, pepper and tomato sauce and stir to combine, then reduce the heat, cover, and continue cooking for 15 minutes. Stir in the hard-boiled egg and pickled gherkin, then remove from the heat and allow to cool before filling the pastry. Taste, and add more seasoning if necessary.

To make the pastry, sift the flour and salt into a bowl. In a separate bowl, combine the sugar, egg yolk and 125 ml (4 fl oz/½ cup) water. Add to the flour and mix well, then knead until smooth. Leave to rest for 15 minutes. Roll out half the pastry very thinly on a lightly floured work surface and brush with half of the melted butter. Roll up tightly into a long, thin roll. Cut into 2.5 cm (1 in) thick slices, then roll each slice out again into a circle with a 10 cm (4 in) diameter.

Put a spoonful of filling in the centre of each circle, brush the edges with the egg white and fold to make a half-moon shape pressing to seal. Repeat with the remaining pastry and filling.

Heat the lard in a large heavy-based frying pan over medium heat. When the oil is hot, deep-fry the empanadas, in batches, until golden brown. Drain on paper towel and serve warm.

Lumpia

Makes: about 24

Egg roll wrappers

5 eggs

1 teaspoon salt

2 tablespoons oil, plus extra for cooking

150 g (5½ oz/1 cup) plain (all-purpose) flour

Lumpia

2 tablespoons peanut oil

4 garlic cloves, finely chopped

1 cooked boneless skinless chicken breast, diced

500 g (1 lb 2 oz/2 cups) diced cooked pork

250 g (1 lb 2 oz/2 cups) diced cooked prawn (shrimp) meat

125 g (4½ oz/1 cup) sliced green beans

90 g (3 oz/1 cup) fresh bean sprouts, trimmed

250 g (9 oz/3⅓ cups) shredded cabbage

140 g (5 oz/1 cup) finely diced celery

30 g (1 oz/½ cup) thinly sliced spring onions (scallions)

2 teaspoons salt

1 teaspoon freshly ground black pepper

2 tablespoons light soy sauce

cos (romaine) lettuce leaves, to serve

Dipping sauce

75 g (2¾ oz/⅓ cup) sugar

60 ml (2 fl oz/¼ cup) light soy sauce

250 ml (8½ fl oz/1 cup) clear chicken stock or water

2 tablespoons cornflour (cornstarch)

1 garlic clove, crushed

¼ teaspoon salt

To make the egg roll wrappers, whisk together the eggs and 375 ml (12½ fl oz/1½ cups) cold water in a bowl until well combined but not too frothy. Add the salt, oil and flour and beat until smooth. Allow to rest for 30 minutes.

Lightly oil a heavy-based frying pan or pancake pan. Pour in a small ladle of the wrapper mixture and swirl to thinly coat the base of the pan. Cook over low heat until the underside is cooked and pale golden. Turn and cook the other side for a few seconds only – these wrappers should not be allowed to brown. Remove to a plate and repeat until all the batter is used – you should make about 25 wrappers in total.

To make the lumpia filling, heat the peanut oil in a wok or large heavy-based frying pan over low heat. Add the garlic and cook for 1 minute, then add the chicken, pork and prawn meat and stir-fry for 1 minute. Add the beans, stir-fry for 2 minutes, then add the bean sprouts, cabbage, celery and spring onion and toss to combine. Continue cooking, stirring often, until the vegetables are tender but still crunchy. Add the salt, pepper and soy sauce and mix well to combine. Remove from the heat and drain off any excess moisture.

To make the dipping sauce, combine the sugar, soy sauce and stock in a saucepan and bring to the boil. In a separate bowl, combine the cornflour and 60 ml (2 fl oz/¼ cup) cold water to make a smooth paste, then add to the pan and stir until the sauce thickens. Continue to simmer for 1 minute, stirring constantly, then stir in the garlic. Remove from the heat and set aside.

To prepare fresh lumpia, put a cos lettuce leaf on an egg roll wrapper. Put 2 tablespoons of filling on the leaf, and roll up so that one end is enclosed and the leaf shows at the other end. Serve at room temperature accompanied by the dipping sauce.

To prepare fried lumpia, do not use the lettuce; instead, put 2 tablespoons of the mixture at one end of an egg roll wrapper and roll up, folding in the sides so that the filling is completely enclosed. Dampen the edges with water and press to seal. Repeat with the remaining wrappers and filling. If not serving immediately, cover and refrigerate until needed.

Heat the oil in a wok or large heavy-based frying pan over medium heat. When the oil is hot, deep-fry the lumpia, in batches, for 2 minutes, or until golden brown and crisp. Drain on paper towel and serve with the sauce.

Fritada
Chicken fritada

Serves: 4–6

....

1 × 1.5 kg (3 lb 5 oz) whole chicken

2 tablespoons lard or oil

5 garlic cloves, crushed

1 large onion, thinly sliced

2 ripe tomatoes, diced

1½ teaspoons salt

½ teaspoon freshly ground black pepper

500 g (1 lb 2 oz) new potatoes, halved or
   quartered if large

1 red capsicum (bell pepper), deseeded and
   thinly sliced

1 green capsicum (bell pepper), deseeded
   and thinly sliced

Chicken stock

neck, back and wings of whole chicken
   (see above)

1 teaspoon salt

1 star anise

whole black peppercorns

1 onion, peeled

1 garlic clove

3–4 celery leaves

1 carrot, chopped

Joint the chicken (see page 12) and cut it into serving pieces. Reserve the neck, back and wing tips for making the stock.

To make the chicken stock, put the reserved neck, back and wing tips into a large saucepan with enough water to cover. Add all the remaining ingredients and simmer over low heat for at least 30 minutes, or longer if you prefer a stronger flavour. Strain and reserve 375 ml (12½ fl oz/1½ cups) of the hot stock.

Heat the lard in a large heavy-based frying pan over low heat. Add the garlic and onion and cook until the onion is soft. Add the chicken and turn to brown on all sides. Add the tomato, salt, pepper and stock, cover, and cook over medium heat until the chicken is half done. Add the potato and capsicums and continue cooking until the potato is done. Serve hot with white rice.

Adobong Manok
Chicken adobo with coconut sauce

Serves: 6

1 × 1.5 kg (3 lb 5 oz) whole chicken

1 tablespoon finely chopped garlic

190 ml (6½ fl oz/¾ cup) white vinegar

1 teaspoon salt

1 bay leaf

½ teaspoon whole peppercorns

3–4 annatto seeds (glossary)

2 tablespoons light soy sauce

oil for frying

125 ml (4 fl oz/½ cup) thick coconut milk
(pages 8–9)

Joint the chicken (see page 12) and cut into serving pieces, separating the drumsticks from thighs and cutting the breast into 4 pieces. Put the chicken into a large saucepan, add the garlic, vinegar, salt, bay leaf, peppercorns, annatto seeds, soy sauce and enough water to cover. Bring to the boil, then reduce the heat to low, cover, and simmer for 25–30 minutes. Uncover, and continue simmering for a further 10 minutes, or until the chicken is tender but not falling off the bone. Remove the chicken pieces to a plate.

Bring the liquid in the pan to the boil and cook quickly until thickened and reduced to about 375 ml (12½ fl oz/1½ cups). Strain into a bowl and refrigerate briefly to cool. Skim as much fat as possible off the sauce.

Heat a little oil in a large heavy-based frying pan and lightly fry the chicken over high heat to brown, then turn to brown the other side.

Meanwhile, heat the sauce in a separate saucepan with the coconut milk, stirring until well combined and heated through. Serve the chicken with the warm sauce spooned over the top and white rice.

Meat

Pipi-An
Chicken and pork in peanut sauce

Serves: 6–8

750 g (1 lb 11 oz) boneless skinless chicken thighs, cut into large cubes

500 g (1 lb 2 oz) pork loin chops (cutlets), cut into large cubes

125 g (4½ oz) ham, diced

salt and freshly ground black pepper

Sauce

100 g (3½ oz/½ cup) long-grain rice

80 g (2¾ oz) lard or 80 ml (2½ fl oz/⅓ cup) oil

1 teaspoon annatto seeds (glossary)

1 garlic clove, crushed

2 onions, finely chopped

2 tablespoons pork fat, diced

125 g (4½ oz/½ cup) peanut butter

Put the chicken, pork and ham into a saucepan with enough water to just cover, and season with salt and freshly ground black pepper. Bring to the boil, then reduce the heat to low and simmer until the meat is tender. Strain the meat, reserving the stock.

To make the sauce, toast the rice in a dry frying pan over low heat until golden, then grind to a powder in a food processor or pound using a mortar and pestle. Heat the lard in a large heavy-based frying pan over low heat. Add the annatto seeds and stir-fry for 1 minute – you will need to cover the pan. Remove the seeds using a skimmer and discard. In the coloured oil, cook the garlic, onion and pork fat until soft and golden brown.

Mix together the ground rice and the reserved stock to make a smooth cream, then add to the pan with the peanut butter, stirring well to combine. Bring to the boil, adding more stock as necessary. Add the chicken, pork and ham to the sauce and continue to cook until heated through. Serve with white rice.

Sotanghon Manok
Chicken with cellophane noodles

Serves: 4–6

250 g (9 oz) cellophane (bean thread) noodles

6 large dried shiitake mushrooms

1 × 1.5 kg (3 lb 5 oz) whole chicken

2 tablespoons lard or oil

1 onion, thinly sliced

2 garlic cloves, crushed

1 tablespoon fish sauce

2 teaspoons annatto seeds (glossary)

12 spring onions (scallions), thinly sliced

Soak the noodles in hot water for 10 minutes, then drain well and cut into short lengths.

Soak the mushrooms in hot water for 20–30 minutes, then drain well, cut off and discard the stems and thinly slice the caps.

Put the chicken into a large heavy-based saucepan with enough water to cover and bring to the boil. Reduce the heat to low, cover, and simmer for 40 minutes, or until the chicken is tender. Allow to cool in the cooking liquid, then lift out the chicken and drain. Remove all the skin and bones from the chicken and cut the meat into large pieces. Strain and reserve the stock.

Heat the lard in a large heavy-based frying pan over low heat. Add the onion and garlic and cook until soft and golden. Add the chicken meat and fish sauce and allow to simmer for a few minutes. Combine the annatto seeds and 2 tablespoons hot water in a bowl and stir until the water turns bright orange, then strain off the water and add to the pan with the reserved chicken stock. Bring to the boil, add the noodles and mushrooms and continue simmering for 15 minutes. Just before serving, stir through the spring onion and season with salt and freshly ground black pepper, to taste. Serve hot.

Meat

Arroz Caldo
Rice with chicken

Serves: 6

1 × 1 kg (3 lb 5 oz) whole chicken

2 tablespoons oil

10 garlic cloves, finely chopped

1 onion, thinly sliced

1 teaspoon finely chopped fresh ginger

495 g (1 lb 1 oz/2¼ cups) short-grain rice

60 ml (2 fl oz/¼ cup) fish sauce

4 spring onions (scallions), thinly sliced

Joint the chicken (see page 12) and cut into serving pieces.

Heat the oil in a wok or large heavy-based frying pan over low heat. Add the garlic and cook until pale golden. Remove to a plate. Add the onion and ginger to the wok and stir-fry until soft, then add the chicken and stir-fry until the chicken is golden and half-cooked. Add the rice and toss to combine for 3 minutes, then return half of the fried garlic to the wok with the fish sauce and 1 litre (34 fl oz/4 cups) water. Bring to the boil, then reduce the heat to low, cover, and simmer for 20 minutes without lifting the lid. Serve garnished with the reserved fried garlic and the spring onion.

Tinola
Chicken tinola

Serves: 4–6

1 × 1.5 kg (3 lb 5 oz) whole chicken

1 tablespoon lard or oil

1 onion, thinly sliced

2 garlic cloves, crushed

1 tablespoon finely grated fresh ginger

1 green papaya, peeled, deseeded and sliced

fish sauce, to taste

freshly ground black pepper, to taste

Joint the chicken (see page 12) and cut into serving pieces.

Heat the lard in a large heavy-based saucepan over low heat. Add the onion, garlic and ginger and cook until soft. Add the chicken and stir-fry until the chicken is well browned. Add 500 ml (17 fl oz/2 cups) water, bring to the boil, then reduce the heat to low, cover, and simmer gently until the chicken is just tender. Add the papaya to the pan and continue to simmer until very tender. Season with fish sauce and freshly ground black pepper to taste and serve immediately.

Pancit Guisado
Fried noodles with mixed meats

Serves: 6–8

500 g (1 lb 2 oz) raw prawns (shrimp)

500 g (1 lb 2 oz) thin egg noodles

60–80 ml (2–2½ fl oz/¼–⅓ cup) oil, plus
  extra for sprinkling

5 garlic cloves, crushed

2 onions, thinly sliced

175 g (6 oz/1 cup) shredded cooked chicken

250 g (9 oz/1 cup) thinly sliced cooked pork

115 g (4 oz/¾ cup) thinly sliced ham,
  cut into fine strips

75 g (2¾ oz/1 cup) shredded cabbage

60 ml (2 fl oz/¼ cup) light soy sauce

lemon wedges, to serve

Put the prawns in a saucepan with enough salted water to cover. Simmer lightly until they turn pink, then remove from the heat and drain the prawns, straining and reserving 250 ml (8½ fl oz/1 cup) of the stock. Peel and devein the prawns and chop into pieces.

Soak the noodles in hot water, then cook the noodles in a saucepan of boiling water until tender. Drain well and spread out in a large baking tray lined with baking paper and dry out for at least 30 minutes, sprinkling a little oil over to prevent them sticking.

Heat 1 tablespoon of the oil in a wok or large heavy-based frying pan over high heat. Add the noodles, a handful at a time, and stir-fry until golden. As each batch is done, remove to a plate, adding more oil to the wok as needed, until all the noodles are cooked.

Heat another 1 tablespoon of the oil. Separately add the garlic, onion, prawn meat, chicken, pork and ham, cooking each until golden and removing to a plate once cooked. Set aside some of each for garnishing the dish, then return everything, except the noodles, to the wok with the cabbage, soy sauce and prawn stock. Add salt and freshly ground black pepper to taste, and toss to combine. Cook until almost dry, then return the noodles to the wok and heat through, tossing well. Arrange on a serving platter and garnish with the reserved ingredients and lemon wedges.

Pochero
Mixed meat stew with vegetables

Serves: 6

This dish is a two-course meal from one pot, rather like the French pot au feu, but featuring mixed meats.

220 g (8 oz/1 cup) dried chickpeas (garbanzo beans)

1 × 1.5 kg (3 lb 5 oz) whole chicken

500 g (1 lb 2 oz) pork, cut into large cubes

2 chorizo (Spanish sausages), cut into 2.5 cm (1 in) slices

1 large onion, sliced

1 tablespoon salt

1 teaspoon whole black peppercorns

80 ml (2½ fl oz/⅓ cup) oil

10 garlic cloves, crushed

1 onion, finely chopped

2 ripe tomatoes, peeled and diced or 410 g (14½ oz/1⅔ cups) tinned diced tomatoes

500 g (1 lb 2 oz) sweet potatoes, peeled and cut into cubes

1 head Chinese cabbage (wombok), cut into 5 cm (2 in) chunks

8 spring onions (scallions), cut into 5 cm (2 in) lengths

Wash the chickpeas and soak overnight in plenty of water.

Joint the chicken (see page 12) and cut into serving pieces.

Put the chicken, pork, chorizo and drained chickpeas into a large heavy-based saucepan. Add the onion, salt and peppercorns and enough water to cover. Bring to the boil, then reduce the heat to low, cover, and simmer until the meat and chickpeas are tender.

Heat the oil in a separate saucepan over low heat. Add the garlic and onion and cook until golden brown. Add the tomato and cook until soft and pulpy, then add to the pan with the meat and stock. Add the sweet potato and simmer until it is half-cooked, then add the cabbage and spring onion and cook for a further 3–4 minutes, or until heated through and just tender. Remove the meat, chickpeas and vegetables from the pan and serve on plates with the broth served separately in a bowl.

Mechado
Beef pot roast

Serves: 6–8

1.5 kg (3 lb 5 oz) beef topside in one piece

strips of pork fat (optional)

4 large onions, quartered

4 large tomatoes, halved

1 bay leaf

125 ml (4 fl oz/½ cup) palm or rice vinegar,
   or diluted white vinegar

1 tablespoon light soy sauce

6 potatoes, peeled and quartered

½ teaspoon freshly ground black pepper

2 tablespoons lard or oil

Use a sharp knife to make cuts in the beef and insert the strips of pork fat at regular intervals, if using – this will help to keep the beef moist. Put the meat in a deep, heavy-based saucepan with the onion, tomato, bay leaf, vinegar, soy sauce and enough water to cover the meat. Bring to the boil, then reduce the heat to low, cover, and simmer until the meat is almost tender. Add the potato and pepper and simmer, uncovered, until the potato is cooked and the liquid almost evaporated.

Transfer the sauce to a serving plate, add the lard to the pan and continue to cook the beef over high heat, turning often, until brown all over. Remove from the pan, cut into slices and serve with the potato and sauce.

Picadillo
Savoury minced beef

Serves: 6

1 tablespoon lard or oil

4 garlic cloves, finely chopped

1 onion, finely chopped

500 g (1 lb 2 oz) minced (ground) beef

2 tomatoes, peeled and chopped

500 ml (17 fl oz/2 cups) beef stock

1 teaspoon salt

¼ teaspoon freshly ground black pepper

500 g (1 lb 2 oz) potatoes, peeled and cubed

Heat the lard in a large heavy-based saucepan over low heat. Add the garlic and onion and cook until soft and golden. Add the beef and stir until the meat has changed colour, then add the tomato and cook until it is soft and pulpy. Add the stock, salt and pepper and bring to the boil. Reduce the heat to low, cover, and simmer for 20 minutes, then add the potato and cook for a further 25 minutes, or until the potato is cooked through. Serve hot.

Sinigang Na Carne
Sour soup of beef

Serves: 6–8

500 g (1 lb 2 oz) beef shin (shank)

500 g (1 lb 2 oz) soup (beef) bones

250 g (9 oz) pork chop (cutlet), trimmed of fat

1 onion, thinly sliced

2 under-ripe tomatoes, sliced

2 teaspoons salt

1 tablespoon tamarind pulp

1 large sweet potato, peeled and diced

1 large daikon (white radish), peeled and sliced

130 g (4½ oz/2 cups) shredded English spinach or other leafy greens

fish sauce, to taste

lime or lemon wedges, to serve

Put the beef, soup bones and pork chop into a large saucepan or stockpot with enough water to cover the meat. Add the onion, tomato and salt. Bring to the boil, then reduce the heat to low, cover, and simmer until the meat is tender. Remove the meat to a plate and allow to cool, then thinly slice the pork and dice the beef. Discard the bones.

Meanwhile, soak the tamarind pulp in 250 ml (8½ fl oz/1 cup) hot water for 10 minutes. Squeeze to dissolve the pulp in the water, then strain, discarding the seeds and fibre.

Return the meat to the soup in the pan. Add the tamarind liquid, sweet potato and radish and continue to simmer over low heat until the vegetables are almost soft, then add the spinach and season with fish sauce, to taste. As soon as the spinach has wilted, serve hot with the lime or lemon wedges.

Beef Pares
Spiced beef stew

Serves: 4

Beef pares is a heady beef stew, fragrant with star anise. Traditionally made with brisket, I prefer to use shin (shank or gravy beef) as it is less fatty, but stays moist because of the connective tissue which turns meltingly gelatinous with long cooking. Don't make the mistake of using a lean cut such as blade (chuck) – it will end up dry as old boots.

500 g (1 lb 2 oz) beef, diced

60 ml (2 fl oz/¼ cup) soy sauce

1 teaspoon freshly ground black pepper

55 g (2 oz/¼ cup) firmly packed soft
  brown sugar

2 onions, 1 chopped, 1 finely chopped

2 star anise

2 tablespoons oil

3 garlic cloves, chopped

3 tablespoons thinly sliced spring onion
  (scallion), to serve

Put the beef, soy sauce, pepper, sugar, chopped onion and star anise in a large saucepan with 1 litre (34 fl oz/4 cups) water. Bring to the boil, then reduce the heat to low and simmer for 1 hour, or until the meat is tender (this will vary depending on the cut used). Allow the meat to cool in the liquid, then lift out the beef and reserve the stock.

Heat the oil in a large heavy-based frying pan over low heat. Add the finely chopped onion and garlic and cook until soft. Add the drained, cooked beef and cook, stirring, for a few minutes, then add the reserved stock and simmer until the liquid has thickened and reduced. Garnish with the spring onion and serve with rice

Morcon
Stuffed rolled beef

Serves: 6–8

1.5 kg (3 lb 5 oz) thick skirt (flank) steak in one piece

1½ teaspoons salt

½ teaspoon freshly ground black pepper

2 tablespoons lemon juice

2 garlic cloves, crushed

2 sweet gherkins (dill pickles), sliced lengthways

2 chorizo (Spanish sausages), sliced lengthways

2 thick slices cooked ham, sliced

2 hard-boiled eggs, cut lengthways into quarters

2 tablespoons lard

2 tablespoons palm or rice vinegar, or 1 tablespoon white vinegar

3 ripe tomatoes, peeled and chopped

Use a sharp knife to cut the steak through the middle, starting at the thickest edge and being careful not to cut through. This should give you a very flat piece of steak almost double the size it was originally. Sprinkle with the salt, pepper and lemon juice and smear with the crushed garlic.

Arrange the pickle, chorizo, ham and hard-boiled egg in rows over the beef, starting at one end, then roll up carefully and tie with kitchen string, so that it is firm but not too tight.

Heat the lard in a large heavy-based frying pan. Add the meat and turn to brown on all sides. Drain off any excess fat, then add the vinegar, tomato and 500 ml (17 fl oz/2 cups) water and bring to the boil. Reduce the heat to low, cover, and simmer gently, for 1¼ hours, or until the meat is tender when tested with a thin metal skewer. Remove the meat to a plate to rest briefly before serving.

Bring the liquid in the pan to a boil and cook rapidly until the sauce thickens. Remove the kitchen string from the rolled beef and cut into slices. Serve hot with the sauce on the side.

Kari-Kari
Beef and vegetable stew

Serves: 6–8

2 kg (4 lb 6 oz) oxtail, jointed

1 kg (2 lb 3 oz) beef shin (shank) on the
 bone, sliced

3 teaspoons salt

60 ml (2 fl oz/¼ cup) vegetable oil

2 teaspoons annatto seeds (glossary)

2 large onions, thinly sliced

4 large garlic cloves, finely chopped

100 g (3½ oz/½ cup) long-grain rice

80 g (2¾ oz/½ cup) roasted peanuts

1 teaspoon freshly ground black pepper

375 g (13 oz/3 cups) sliced green beans

2 eggplants (aubergines), cut into
 large pieces

2 tablespoons fish sauce, or to taste

2 tablespoons thinly sliced spring onion
 (scallion), to garnish

2 tablespoons chopped celery leaves,
 to garnish

Put the oxtail and beef into a pressure cooker with just enough water to cover. Add 2 teaspoons of the salt and cook under pressure for 1 hour. Allow to cool to lukewarm, then strain the stock, reserving the meat. Put the stock in the refrigerator to chill. If no pressure cooker is available, simmer the meat in a large saucepan until almost tender.

Wipe the meat with paper towel to soak up any excess moisture. Heat 1 tablespoon of the oil in a large heavy-based saucepan or casserole dish and brown the pieces of meat, turning regularly, until brown all over – you may need to do this in batches. Remove to a plate when done.

Pour the fat from the pan and heat the remaining oil over low heat. Add the annatto seeds and stir-fry over low heat for 1 minute – you may need to cover the pan as they might spit. Remove the seeds using a slotted spoon and discard. Add the onion and garlic and cook in the coloured oil until soft.

Remove the top layer of fat from the chilled stock and re-heat it in a small saucepan until liquid, then stir in 2 litres (68 fl oz/8 cups) hot water to combine.

Put the rice in a dry frying pan and cook over medium heat, stirring frequently, until the grains are evenly coloured. When they are deep golden, allow to cool slightly, then grind to a powder in a spice grinder or food processor. Add the peanuts and continue to process to a powder.

Return the meat to the pan with the onion and garlic and stir to combine, then add the water mixture and pepper and bring to the boil. Reduce the heat to low, partially cover, and simmer until the meat is tender and easily pierced with a fork, but not falling off the bone. There should be enough liquid to cover the meat; if not, add more hot water. Add the rice powder, stirring until smooth. Add the beans and eggplant and simmer for 10 minutes, or until the vegetables are tender. Add the fish sauce to taste.

Serve immediately, garnished with the spring onion and celery leaves with white rice on the side. If liked, accompany this dish with extra fish sauce, soy sauce, a hot sambal sauce or (for real Filipino eating) a sauce made from equal quantities of shrimp paste and lime juice.

Menudo
Pork and liver stew

Serves: 6

1 tablespoon oil

2 teaspoons annatto seeds (glossary)

1 tablespoon crushed garlic

1 onion, finely chopped

2 tomatoes, sliced

500 g (1 lb 2 oz) pork, cut into 5 cm
    (2 in) cubes

3 potatoes, diced

250 g (9 oz) pork liver, finely diced

2 teaspoons salt

½ teaspoon freshly ground black pepper

Heat the oil in a large heavy-based saucepan over low heat. Add the annatto seeds and stir-fry for 1 minute, then lift out the seeds with a slotted spoon and discard.

Add the garlic and onion to the coloured oil in the pan and cook until soft and golden. Add the tomato and cook until soft and pulpy, then add the pork, cover, and bring to the boil. Reduce the heat to low and simmer until the pork is tender. Add the potato – you may need to add a little stock or water at this point if there is very little liquid in the pan. Simmer until the potato is cooked through. Add the liver to the pan with the salt and pepper and bring back to the boil until the liver is cooked through. Serve hot.

Almondigas (1)
Beef and pork balls simmered in stock

Serves: 4

250 g (9 oz) minced (ground) pork

250 g (9 oz) minced (ground) beef

1 teaspoon salt

1 teaspoon freshly ground black pepper

1 small egg

1½ tablespoons oil

2 garlic cloves, finely chopped

1 onion, finely chopped

2 ripe tomatoes, diced

1 litre (34 fl oz/4 cups) rice water (see note)

2 teaspoons soy sauce

In a large bowl, combine the pork and beef, salt, pepper and egg, using your hands to mix well. Take portions of the mixture at a time and shape into balls.

Heat the oil in a large heavy based frying pan over low heat. Add the garlic and onion and cook until golden brown, then add the tomato and cook, stirring often, until soft. Add the rice water, bring to the boil, then add the meatballs, in batches, and simmer until well cooked. Serve hot.

Note

'Rice water' is the water in which rice has been washed prior to cooking.

Almondigas (2)
Pork and prawn balls

Serves: 4

250 g (9 oz) raw prawns (shrimp), peeled, deveined and finely chopped

250 g (9 oz) minced (ground) pork

1 spring onion (scallion), finely chopped

½ teaspoon salt

1 tablespoon oil

1 onion, finely chopped

2 garlic cloves, crushed

½ teaspoon shrimp sauce

salt and freshly ground black pepper, to taste

½ cup fine wheat noodles

In a large bowl, combine the prawn meat, pork, spring onion and salt, and use your hands to mix well. Take portions of the mixture at a time and shape into balls.

Heat the oil in a large heavy-based frying pan over low heat. Add the onion and garlic and cook until golden brown, then add the shrimp sauce and 750 ml (25½ fl oz/3 cups) water. Bring to the boil, then add the meatballs, in batches, and cook for 8 minutes, or until well cooked. Return all the balls to the pan and add the noodles, then remove from the heat, cover, and allow to stand for 5 minutes. Season with salt and freshly ground black pepper, to taste, and serve hot.

Note

You can use rice vermicelli (rice-stick) noodles instead of the fine wheat noodles, but you will need to cook them for 1 minute before removing from the heat.

Adobong Baboy
Pork adobo

Serves: 6

1 kg (2 lb 3 oz) pork loin chops or leg chops (cutlets)

8–10 garlic cloves

500 ml (17 fl oz/2 cups) palm or rice vinegar, or 250 ml (8½ fl oz/1 cup) white vinegar diluted in 250 ml (8½ fl oz/1 cup) water

2 bay leaves

1½ teaspoons salt

1 teaspoon freshly ground black pepper

oil for frying

Cut the skin from the pork and discard. If the chops are large, cut into serving pieces. Put the pork, garlic, vinegar, bay leaves, salt and pepper into a large heavy-based saucepan and toss well to combine. Set aside to marinate for 1 hour.

Place the pan over high heat and bring to the boil, then reduce the heat to low and simmer for 40 minutes, or until the pork is tender. Remove the pork to a plate.

Increase the heat to high and continue to boil the sauce over high heat until reduced and thickened. Strain into a small bowl, spoon off the fat and return it to the pan. Add enough oil to cover the base of the pan in 5 mm (¼ in) fat. Add the pork and cook, turning often, until evenly brown and crisp all over. Serve with the sauce over the top and white rice on the side.

Variation

To make a chicken and pork adobo use 500 g (1 lb 2 oz) pork and 1 × 1.25 kg (2 lb 12 oz) whole chicken. Joint the chicken (see page 12) and cut into serving pieces. Follow the method above, but reduce the simmering time to 30 minutes. Serve garnished with pimiento strips or tomato wedges, with white rice on the side.

Umba

Simmered pork

Serves: 6

1 kg (2 lb 3 oz) pork shoulder, cut into
    large cubes

2 garlic cloves, finely chopped

2 tablespoons soy sauce

2 tablespoons soft brown sugar

1 teaspoon salt

125 ml (4 fl oz/½ cup) palm or rice vinegar,
    or diluted white vinegar

½ bay leaf

Put the pork into a large heavy-based saucepan with 250 ml (8½ fl oz/1 cup) water. Add all the remaining ingredients and bring to the boil, then reduce the heat to low, cover, and simmer until the pork is cooked through and tender. Serve with rice.

Vegetables

Rellenong Talong
Stuffed eggplant

Serves: 4

2 eggplants (aubergines), halved lengthways

2 teaspoons salt

1 tablespoon oil

3 garlic cloves, finely chopped

1 onion, finely chopped

250 g (9 oz) minced (ground) pork

1 large ripe tomato, chopped

1 teaspoon freshly ground black pepper

80 g (2¾ oz/1 cup) fresh breadcrumbs

1 egg, beaten

dry breadcrumbs for coating

oil for frying

Put the eggplant and 250 ml (8½ fl oz/1 cup) water in a saucepan with 1 teaspoon of the salt. Bring to the boil, then reduce the heat to low and simmer until tender but not too soft. Remove the eggplant from the water and place over paper towel, cut sides down, to drain. Scoop out some of the flesh, leaving a firm shell. Finely chop the flesh and set aside.

Heat the oil in a large heavy-based frying pan over low heat. Add the garlic and onion and cook until golden. Add the pork and stir-fry until it changes colour. Add the tomato, pepper and remaining salt and cook for 15 minutes. Add the eggplant pulp and continue cooking until the mixture starts to dry out. Remove from the heat, stir in the fresh breadcrumbs, taste and season with salt and freshly ground black pepper, if desired.

Divide the mixture among the eggplant halves to fill each one, then brush over the tops with the egg and scatter over the dry breadcrumbs to coat.

Heat the oil in a large heavy-based saucepan over medium heat. Add the eggplants and cook on one side for 10 minutes, before gently turning and cooking the top until golden. Serve hot.

Ampalaya
Bitter melon with prawns

Serves: 6

500 g (1 lb 2 oz) bitter melons (gourds)

250 g (9 oz) raw prawns (shrimp)

oil for frying

2 onions, chopped

5 garlic cloves, chopped

250 g (9 oz) pork fillet, thinly sliced

1 kg (2 lb 3 oz) ripe tomatoes, peeled and chopped

125 ml (4 fl oz/½ cup) palm or rice vinegar

Cut the bitter melons in half lengthways, scoop out and discard the seeds and thinly slice.

Put the prawns and 500 ml (17 fl oz/2 cups) water in a saucepan with a little salt over medium heat and cook lightly until they turn pink. Allow to cool, then drain the prawns, straining and reserving 250 ml (8½ fl oz/1 cup) of the stock. Peel and devein the prawns and chop into small pieces.

Heat the oil in a large heavy-based frying pan over medium heat. Add the onion and garlic and cook until golden. Add the pork and stir-fry until the colour changes, then add the tomato and cook until soft and pulpy. Add the prawn meat and reserved stock and stir well, then bring to the boil. Reduce the heat to low, add the vinegar and simmer for 3–4 minutes. Add the bitter melon and continue simmering, or until the melon is tender. Season with salt and freshly ground black pepper to taste, and serve hot with white rice.

Amargoso Salad
Bitter melon salad

Serves: 4

....

1 bitter melon (gourd), thinly sliced

250 g (9 oz) raw prawns (shrimp)

2 firm red tomatoes, peeled and diced

2 hard-boiled eggs, chopped

Dressing

60 ml (2 fl oz/¼ cup) white vinegar

½ teaspoon salt

2 teaspoons sugar

¼ teaspoon freshly ground black pepper

Blanch the bitter melon in a saucepan of boiling water for 1 minute, then drain immediately and cool.

Put the prawns and 500 ml (17 fl oz/2 cups) water in a saucepan with a little salt over medium heat and cook lightly until they turn pink. Allow to cool, then drain well. Peel and devein the prawns and chop into pieces. Allow to cool.

Put the bitter melon, prawn meat, tomato and hard-boiled egg into a large serving bowl.

In a small bowl, combine all the dressing ingredients, stirring well to dissolve the sugar. Pour over the salad and toss gently to coat. Cover and chill before serving.

Salad Na Papaya
Papaya salad

Serves: 6

....

1 firm papaya

1 small ripe pineapple, peeled, cored and diced

2 spring onions (scallions), thinly sliced

1 apple, peeled, cored and diced

60 g (2 oz/½ cup) thinly sliced celery

125 ml (4 fl oz/½ cup) salad dressing or mayonnaise

Peel the papaya, cut in halves and scoop out the seeds. Cut the flesh into dice. Combine the papaya in a large serving bowl with the pineapple, spring onion, apple and celery. Add the salad dressing and toss to coat all the ingredients. Season with salt and freshly ground black pepper, to taste, then cover and chill before serving.

Sweets
and
Desserts

Capuchinos
Small brandied cakes

Makes: 12

60 g (2 oz) butter, melted, plus extra for greasing

75 g (2¾ oz/½ cup) plain (all-purpose) flour

½ teaspoon baking powder

a pinch of salt

2 large eggs

110 g (4 oz/½ cup) sugar

1 tablespoon brandy

Syrup

110 g (4 oz/½ cup) sugar

1 tablespoon brandy

Preheat the oven to 200°C (400°F). Lightly grease a 12-hole muffin tray with the extra butter.

To make the syrup, put the sugar and 125 ml (4 fl oz/½ cup) water into a small saucepan over low heat and stir to dissolve the sugar. Bring to the boil and boil for 2 minutes, then remove from the heat and allow to cool before stirring in the brandy.

Sift together the flour, baking powder and salt in a bowl.

Beat the eggs in a separate bowl until frothy, add the sugar gradually and continue beating until thick and light. Mix in the melted butter and brandy, then fold in the dry ingredients until well combined.

Half-fill each muffin hole with batter and bake for about 10–12 minutes, or until the cakes are golden brown. Remove from the muffin holes, and while still warm, dip briefly into the syrup to coat and place on a wire rack to cool and dry before serving.

Ensaimada
Sweet bread rolls

Makes: 18

30 g (1 oz) fresh compressed yeast

3 teaspoons sugar

600 g (1 lb 5 oz/4 cups) plain (all-purpose) flour

185 g (6½ oz) butter, plus 125 g (4½ oz) extra, melted

115 g (4 oz/½ cup) caster (superfine) sugar, plus 3 tablespoons extra for sprinkling

6 egg yolks

125 ml (4 fl oz/½ cup) milk

165 g (6 oz/1¼ cups) finely grated mature cheese, preferably Dutch edam

Crumble the yeast into a bowl with 60 ml (2 fl oz/¼ cup) warm water and stir in the sugar until dissolved. Add 1 teaspoon of the flour and stir to combine, then set aside in a warm place.

Beat the butter until soft, then add the sugar and continue beating until pale and creamy. Add the egg yolks, one at a time, beating well after each addition. Stir in the flour and milk alternately, until combined, then add the yeast mixture and beat well until smooth and combined – the dough should be soft, but not so soft that it sticks to the sides of the bowl; add a little more flour if needed. Roll the dough into a ball. Place in a lightly greased bowl, cover, and leave in a warm place for about 1 hour, or until doubled in size.

Preheat the oven to 170°C (340°F). Grease 2 baking trays. Divide the dough into 2 equal portions and roll out each on a lightly floured work surface to a 45 × 38 cm (18 × 16 in) rectangle. Brush with some of the melted butter and sprinkle with the grated cheese. Cut each rectangle into 3 strips lengthways and roll up each strip like a Swiss (jelly) roll, starting at the long end. Slice each roll into thirds.

Using your hands, roll each piece on the work surface until as thin as a pencil, then form into snail-like coils or twists. Put on the prepared trays, leaving spaces between each, then cover and leave in a warm place for 30–40 minutes, or until doubled in size.

Bake in the oven for 10–12 minutes, or until golden brown. Remove from the oven, and while still hot, brush over the remaining melted butter and sprinkle with caster sugar. Serve ensaimadas warm or at room temperature.

Leche Flan
Caramel custard

Serves: 6–8

110 g (4 oz/½ cup) sugar

3 large eggs

2 egg yolks

115 g (4 oz/½ cup) caster (superfine) sugar

625 ml (21 fl oz/2½ cups) hot milk

2 teaspoons natural vanilla extract

Preheat the oven to 150°C (300°F).

Put the sugar and 60 ml (2 fl oz/¼ cup) water into a small saucepan and heat without stirring until a deep golden brown. Remove from the heat and pour immediately into a 1.5 litre (51 fl oz/6 cup) capacity ovenproof mould or dish. Rotate to coat the base and side with caramel.

In a large bowl, beat together the whole eggs and egg yolks until foamy. Gradually add the caster sugar, beating until thick and light. Gradually add the hot milk, beating constantly. Stir in the vanilla, then strain the custard into the caramel-lined mould.

Put the mould into a deep baking tin and pour in enough boiling water to come halfway up the side of the mould. Bake in the oven for 35–45 minutes, or until a knife inserted into the centre of the custard comes out clean. Remove from the oven and cool, then cover and refrigerate overnight, or preferably for 2 days. When ready to serve, invert the custard onto a chilled serving plate.

Bombones De Arroz
Rice fritters

Makes: about 24

165 g (6 oz/¾ cup) short-grain rice

2 large eggs, lightly beaten

115 g (4 oz/½ cup) caster (superfine) sugar

½ teaspoon natural vanilla extract

½ teaspoon freshly grated nutmeg

110 g (4 oz/¾ cup) plain (all-purpose) flour

3 teaspoons baking powder

oil for deep-frying

icing (confectioners') sugar for sprinkling

Put the rice and 375 ml (12½ fl oz/1½ cups) water in a saucepan over medium heat and bring to the boil. Reduce the heat to low and simmer for 20 minutes, or until the water has been absorbed. Remove from the heat and allow to cool.

In a large bowl, mix together the rice, egg, sugar, vanilla and nutmeg.

Sift together the flour and baking powder in a separate bowl and stir into the rice mixture until thoroughly combined.

Heat the oil in a large heavy-based frying pan over medium heat. Drop 1 tablespoon of the mixture into the hot oil at a time and deep-fry in batches, turning often, until golden brown and nicely puffed. Remove with a slotted spoon and drain on paper towel. Sprinkle with the icing sugar and serve warm.

Note

You can use left-over rice to make these fritters – use 370 g (13 oz/2 cups) cooked rice.

Sweets and Desserts

Mangang Sorbetes
Mango ice cream

Serves: 6

Ice creams made from fruit, coconut and purple yam are popular in the Philippines.

500 ml (17 fl oz/2 cups) milk

2 eggs, separated

115 g (4 oz/½ cup) caster (superfine) sugar

1 teaspoon gelatine

280–370 g (10–13 oz/1½–2 cups) fresh or tinned mango pulp

250 ml (8½ fl oz/1 cup) pouring (single/light) cream

Put the milk into a saucepan and bring slowly to the boil.

Beat the egg yolks with half of the sugar in a bowl, until thick and light. Pour a little of the hot milk onto the yolks, stirring constantly, then add the yolk mixture to the pan and cook over low heat, stirring constantly – do not allow it to reach simmering point or the custard will curdle. As soon as it is thick enough to lightly coat the back of a spoon, remove from the heat and keep stirring until it cools slightly. Pour into a freezer tray and freeze until mushy.

Sprinkle the gelatine over 2 tablespoons cold water in a cup and stand the cup in a small saucepan of water. Bring to the boil so the gelatine dissolves. Put the mango pulp in a bowl and add the gelatine water, stirring to combine.

Whip the cream until it holds soft peaks – do not overbeat or the ice cream will have a buttery texture.

Beat the egg whites until soft peaks form, then add the remaining sugar and beat until soft and glossy.

Scrape the half-frozen custard into a bowl and beat with a hand-held beater until it is smooth, but do not let it melt. (Chilling the bowl helps in hot weather.) Fold in the mango pulp, egg whites and whipped cream and return to the freezer to freeze until firm.

Guava Jelly

Makes: about 1 litre (34 fl oz/4 cups)

2 kg (4 lb 6 oz) slightly under-ripe guavas

4 granny smith apples

sugar

lemon juice

Wash the fruit and cut into quarters. Put into a large saucepan with just enough cold water to cover. Bring to the boil, then reduce the heat to low and simmer for about 1 hour, or until the fruit is soft and loses its colour. Strain into a bowl, through 2 or 3 layers of muslin (cheesecloth) – do not squeeze or the jelly will not be sparkling and clear. Wet the muslin and wring it out before pouring the fruit into it, or a lot of juice will be absorbed by the cloth. Reserve the pulp for making guava paste (see below).

Measure the strained juice and cook no more than 1–1.25 litres (34–42 fl oz/4–5 cups) at a time. Allow 165 g (6 oz/¾ cup) sugar to each cup of juice. Bring to the boil, add the warmed sugar and about 2 tablespoons strained lemon juice and stir until the sugar has dissolved. Cook the jelly, without stirring, skimming off any froth that rises to the top, until the jelly has set. To test, take a spoonful of the liquid, cool slightly and pour back into the pan from the side of the spoon – when it no longer runs off in a steady stream but thickens and 'sheets' as it falls, it is ready. Pour the jelly into sterilised airtight jars.

Membrillo
Guava paste

To make guava paste, follow the recipe above, but after straining the fruit pulp to extract the juice, use the left-over fruit pulp to make a sweetmeat. Push the pulp through a fine nylon sieve, discarding the seeds and skins. Weigh the pulp and allow three-quarters of its weight in sugar. Heat the pulp and sugar with the juice of 1 lemon and stir constantly until very thick. Use a long-handled wooden spoon and cook over very low heat. Take care because as the mixture thickens it may spit. Cook and stir until the mixture is stiff and comes away from the pan in one mass. Turn into a buttered dish, flatten with a buttered spoon and leave to cool and firm up. Cut into thin slices to serve.

Glossary
and Index

Annatto seeds

Botanical name: *Bixa orellana*

These small red seeds are used for colouring and flavouring Filipino food. (They are also used for dyeing silk.) Substitute paprika and turmeric in given amounts (see The Philippines introduction, page 120). Also known as: *achuete* or *atsuete* (Philippines), *hot dieu mau* (Vietnam).

Aromatic ginger

See galangal, lesser.

Asafoetida

Botanical name: *Ferula asafoetida*

Used in minute quantities in Indian cooking. It is obtained from the resinous gum of a plant that grows in Afghanistan and Iran. The stalks are cut close to the root and the milky fluid that flows out is dried into the resin sold as asafoetida. Although it has quite an unpleasant smell by itself, traditionally a tiny piece the size of a pea is attached to the inside of the lid of a cooking pot – this adds depth of flavour and is said to prevent flatulence. If you cannot get the actual resin, use the powdered form, which has been mixed with ground rice, and add with other spices. Also known as: *sheingho* (Burma), *hing* or *perunkaya* (India).

Bamboo shoots

Sold in tins and jars, either water-packed, pickled or braised. Unless otherwise stated, the recipes in this book use the water-packed variety. If using the tinned variety, store left-over bamboo shoots in a bowl of fresh water in the refrigerator, changing the water daily for up to 10 days. Winter bamboo shoots are much smaller and more tender, and are called for in certain recipes. However, if they are not available, use the larger variety. Also known as: *wah-bho-khmyit* (Burma), *tumpeang* (Cambodia), *suehn* (China), *rebung* (Indonesia), *takenoko* (Japan), *rebong* (Malaysia), *labong* (Philippines), *normai* (Thailand), *mang* (Vietnam).

Bean sprouts

Green mung beans are traditionally used for bean sprouts. They are sold fresh in most large supermarkets, Asian grocery stores and health food stores. Chinese stores sell longer shoots than those available from supermarkets, which are usually just starting to sprout. Substitute thinly sliced celery for a similar texture but different flavour. Very fresh bean sprouts can be stored in the refrigerator for up to 4 days in a plastic bag; alternatively, cover with water and change the water daily. Before using, rinse the sprouts, drain well and trim off the brown tails. Also known as: *pepinauk* (Burma), *nga choi* (China), *taoge* (Indonesia), *moyashi* (Japan), *suk ju* (Korea), *taugeh* (Malaysia and Singapore), *tau ngork* (Thailand), *gia* (Vietnam).

Bitter melon (gourd)

Botanical name: *Momordica charantia*

Known variously as bitter melon, bitter gourd, bitter cucumber and balsam pear, this vaguely reptilian-looking vegetable with a warty green exterior should be purchased while young and shiny-skinned. Do not store more than a day or two and even then in the refrigerator, or it will continue to mature. Over-ripe specimens will yellow and their seeds will become very hard. Cultures all over Asia believe this vegetable has powerful medicinal benefits. Also known as: *kyethinkhathee* (Burma), *fu gwa*, *foo kwa* (China), *karela* (India), *pare*, *peria* (Indonesia), *niga-uri* (Japan), *maha* (Laos), *peria* (Malaysia), *ampalaya* (Philippines), *karavila* (Sri Lanka), *bai mara* (Thailand), *kho qua* (Vietnam).

Bombay duck

Not a bird, despite its name, this is a variety of fish that is salted and dried. It is sold in packets and should be cut into pieces no more than 2.5 cm (1 in) long before using. Deep-fried or grilled, it is served as an accompaniment to a meal of rice and curry, and should be nibbled in little pieces.

Cardamom

Botanical name: *Elettaria cardamomum*

Next to saffron, cardamom is the world's most expensive spice. Cardamoms grow mainly in India and Sri Lanka, and are the seed pods of a member of the ginger family. The dried seed pods are either pale green or brown, according to variety; sometimes they are bleached white. They are added, either whole or bruised, to pilaus and other rice dishes, spiced curries and other preparations or sweets. When ground cardamom is called for, the seed pods are opened and discarded and only the small black or brown seeds are ground. For full flavour, it is best to grind them just before using. If you cannot buy a high-quality ground cardamom, crush the seeds using a mortar and pestle or spice mill, as required. Also known as: *phalazee* (Burma), *illaichi* (India), *kapulaga* (Indonesia), *buah pelaga* (Malaysia), *enasal* (Sri Lanka), *kravan* (Thailand).

Cellophane (bean thread) noodles

These are fine, translucent noodles made from the starch of green mung beans. The noodles may be soaked in hot water before use, or may require boiling according to the texture required. They can also be deep-fried straight from the packet, generally when used as a garnish or to provide a background for other foods. Also known as: *kyazan* (Burma), *mee sooer* (Cambodia), *bi fun, ning fun, sai fun, fun see* (China), *sotanghoon* (Indonesia), *harusame* (Japan), *sohoon, tunghoon* (Malaysia), *sotanghon* (Philippines), *woon sen* (Thailand), *búng u, mien* (Vietnam).

Chillies, green and red

Botanical name: *Capsicum* spp.

Chillies mature from green to red, becoming hotter as they mature. Both varieties are used fresh for flavouring, either whole or finely chopped, sliced as a garnish or ground into sambals. The seeds, which are the hottest parts, are usually (though not always) removed. Larger varieties tend to be milder than the small varieties. See page 9 for handling. Dried red chillies are found in packets in Asian grocery stores – the medium- to large-sized chillies are best for most recipes in this book.

Chilli powder

Asian chilli powder is made from ground chillies. It is much hotter than the Mexican-style chilli powder, which is mostly ground cumin. You may be able to find ground Kashmiri chillies, which are a brighter red colour and not as hot as other ground chillies.

Chow chow preserves

A mixture of fruits and vegetables in a heavy syrup, flavoured with ginger, which is also one of the ingredients. Sold in tins or jars, it keeps indefinitely in the refrigerator after opening.

Cinnamon

Botanical name: *Cinnamomum zeylanicum* and *verum*
True cinnamon is native to Sri Lanka. Buy cinnamon sticks or quills rather than the ground spice, which loses its flavour when stored too long. It is used in both sweet and savoury dishes. Cassia, which is grown in India, Indonesia and Burma, is similar. It is much stronger in flavour, and is cheaper, but it lacks the delicacy of cinnamon. The leaves and buds of the cassia tree have a flavour similar to the bark and are also used for flavouring food. For sweet dishes, use true cinnamon. Cassia bark is much thicker because the corky layer is left on. Also known as: *thit-ja-boh-guak* (Burma), *darchini* (India), *kayu manis* (Malaysia and Indonesia), *kurundu* (Sri Lanka), *op chery* (Thailand), *que* (Vietnam).

Cloves

Botanical name: *Syzygium aromaticum*, *Eugenia aromatica* and *E. caryophyllus*
Cloves are the dried flower buds of an evergreen tropical tree native to Southeast Asia. They were used in China more than 2000 years ago, and were also used by the Romans. Oil of cloves contains phenol, a powerful antiseptic that discourages putrefaction, and the clove is hence one of the spices that helps preserve food. Also known as: *ley-nyin-bwint* (Burma), *laung* (India), *cengkeh* (Indonesia), *bunga cingkeh* (Malaysia), *karabu* (Sri Lanka), *kaan ploo* (Thailand).

Coconut milk

This is not the water inside the nut, as is commonly believed, but the creamy liquid extracted from the grated flesh of fresh coconuts or from desiccated (shredded) coconut (pages 8–9). When coconut milk is called for, especially in sweet dishes, do make an effort to use it, for its flavour cannot be duplicated by using any other kind of milk. Tinned and Tetra Pak coconut milk saves time and effort, although be warned that some brands are far better than others so try a few until you find one that appeals. Low-fat coconut milk is an unappealing substitute.

Coriander (cilantro)

Botanical name: *Coriandrum sativum*
All parts of the coriander (cilantro) plant are used in Asian cooking. The dried seed is the main ingredient in curry powder, and although not hot it has a fragrance that makes it an essential part of a curry blend. The fresh coriander herb is also known as cilantro or Chinese parsley in other parts of the world. It is indispensable in Burma, Thailand, Vietnam, Cambodia, India and China where it is also called 'fragrant green'. Also known as: *nannamzee* (seed), *nannambin* (leaves) (Burma), *chee van soy* (Cambodia), *yuen sai* (China), *dhania* (seed), *dhania pattar*, *dhania sabz* (leaves) (India), *phak hom pom* (Laos), *ketumbar* (seeds), *daun ketumbar* (leaves) (Malaysia), *kinchay* (Philippines), *kottamalli* (seed), *kottamalli kolle* (leaves) (Sri Lanka), *pak chee* (Thailand), *ngò*, *rau mùi* (Vietnam).

Cumin

Botanical name: *Cuminum cyminum*
Cumin is, with coriander, the most essential ingredient in prepared curry powders. It is available as seed, or ground. There may be some confusion between cumin and caraway seeds because they are similar in appearance, but the flavours are completely different and one cannot replace the other in recipes. Also known as: *ma-ch'in* (China), *sufaid zeera* (white cumin), *zeera*, *jeera* (India), *jinten* (Indonesia), *kumin* (Japan), *jintan puteh* (Malaysia), *sududuru* (Sri Lanka), *yira* (Thailand).

Curry leaves

Botanical name: *Murraya koenigii*
Sold fresh or dried, they are as important to curries as bay leaves are to stews, but never try to substitute one for the other. The tree is native to Asia, the leaves are small, pointed and shiny, growing in opposing pairs along a central stalk. Although they keep their flavour well when dried or frozen, they are found in such abundance in Asia that they are generally used fresh. The tree is easy to grow from seed even in a temperate climate. The leaves are fried in oil until crisp at the start of preparing a curry. Dried curry leaves can be pulverised using a mortar and pestle; and the powdered leaves can be used in marinades and omelettes. Also known as: *pyi-naw-thein* (Burma), *kitha neem*, *katnim*, *karipattar*, *karuvepila* (India), *daun kari*, *karupillay* (Malaysia), *karapincha* (Sri Lanka).

Curry powder

Rarely used in countries where curry is eaten daily (the word comes from the Tamil kari, meaning 'sauce'). It is preferable to roast and grind the spices separately. For Sri Lankan recipes, be sure to use curry powder that is labelled 'Ceylon curry powder'.

Daikon

Botanical name: *Raphanus sativus*
Daikon (white radish) is a very large white radish most popularly known by its Japanese name. It is about 30–38 cm (12–15¼ in) long with a mild flavour. It is sold in Asian grocery stores and some large greengrocers and supermarkets. Substitute white turnip if not available. Also known as: *loh hahk* (China), *muuli* (India), *lobak* (Indonesia and Malaysia), *mu* (*moo*) (Korea), *labanos* (Philippines), *rabu* (Sri Lanka), *phakkat-hua* (Thailand), *cù cùi trng* (Vietnam).

Daun pandan

See pandanus or screwpine.

Dried fish (sprats)

Salting and drying fish is a common way of preserving fish throughout Asia. Some are small, such as tiny sprats or anchovies. These tiny sprats or anchovies should be rinsed before use. Avoid soaking them, or they will not retain their crispness when fried. Dry on paper towel before frying. Larger salted and dried fish, such as karavadu, are used in main dishes. Also known as: *nga chauk* (Burma), *nethali* (India), *ikan bilis* (Indonesia and Malaysia), *dilis* (Philippines), *haal masso* (Sri Lanka), *plasroi* (Thailand).

Glossary ◆

Fennel

Botanical name: *Foeniculum vulgare*

Sometimes known as 'sweet cumin' or 'large cumin', because of its similar-shaped seeds, it is a member of the same botanical family and is used in Sri Lankan curries (but in much smaller quantities than true cumin). It is available in ground or seed form. Substitute an equal amount of aniseed. Also known as: *samouk-saba* (Burma), *sonf* (India), *adas* (Indonesia), *jintan manis* (Malaysia), *maduru* (Sri Lanka), *yira* (Thailand).

Fenugreek

Botanical name: *Trigonella foenum-graecum*

These small, flat, squarish, brownish-beige seeds are essential in curries, but because they have a slightly bitter flavour they must be used in the stated quantities. They are especially good in fish and seafood curries, where the whole seeds are gently fried at the start of cooking; they are also ground and added to curry powders. The green leaves are used in Indian cooking and, when spiced, the bitter taste is quite piquant and acceptable. The plant is easy to grow and, when at the two-leaf stage, the sprouts make a tangy addition to salads. Also known as: *methi* (India), *alba* (Malaysia), *uluhaal* (Sri Lanka).

Fish sauce

A thin, salty, brown sauce used in Southeast Asian cooking to bring out the flavour in other foods. A small variety of fish is packed in wooden barrels with salt, and the liquid that runs off is the 'fish sauce'. There are different grades of fish sauce, the Vietnamese version being darker and having a more pronounced fish flavour than the others. Also known as: *ngan-pya-ye* (Burma), *tuck trey* (Cambodia), *nam pa* (Laos), *patis* (Philippines), *nam pla* (Thailand), *nuoc nam* (Vietnam).

Galangal, lesser (aromatic ginger)

Botanical name: *Kaempferia pandurata, Alpinia officinarum*

Also known as 'aromatic ginger', this member of the ginger family cannot be used as a substitute for ginger or vice versa. It is used only in certain dishes and gives a pronounced aromatic flavour. When available fresh, it is sliced or pounded to a pulp; but outside of Asia it is usually sold dried, and the hard round slices must be pounded using a mortar and pestle or pulverised in a food processor before use. In some spice ranges it is sold in powdered form as kencur powder. The plant is native to southern China and has been used for centuries in medicinal herbal mixtures, but it is not used in Chinese cooking. Also known as: *sa leung geung, sha geung fun* (China), *kencur* (Indonesia), *zeodary* or *kencur* (Malaysia), *ingurupiyali* (Sri Lanka), *krachai* (Thailand).

Ghee (clarified butter)

Sold in tins, ghee is pure butterfat without any of the milk solids. It can be heated to much higher temperatures than butter without burning, and imparts a distinctive flavour when used as a cooking medium.

Ginger

Botanical name: *Zingiber officinale*

A rhizome with a robust flavour and a warming quality, it is essential in most Asian dishes. Fresh ginger root should be used; powdered ginger cannot be substituted for fresh ginger, for the flavour is quite different. To prepare for use, scrape off the skin with a sharp knife and either grate or chop finely (according to recipe requirements) before measuring. To preserve fresh ginger for long periods of time, place in a freezer bag and store in the freezer – it is a simple matter to peel and grate in the frozen state. Also known as: *gin* (Burma), *khnyahee* (Cambodia), *jeung* (China), *adrak* (India), *jahe* (Indonesia), *shoga* (Japan), *halia* (Malaysia), *luya* (Philippines), *inguru* (Sri Lanka), *khing* (Thailand), *gung* (Vietnam).

Gourd, bitter

See bitter melon.

Ground Rice

See rice, ground

Kencur (aromatic ginger) powder

See Galangal, lesser (aromatic ginger).

Lemongrass

Botanical name: *Cymbopogon citratus*

This aromatic Asian plant is a tall grass with sharp-edged leaves that multiply into clumps. The whitish, slightly bulbous base is used to impart a lemony flavour to curries, salads and soups. Cut just one stem with a sharp knife, close to the root, and use about 10–12 cm (4–4¾ in) of the stalk from the base, discarding the leaves. If you have to use dried lemongrass, about 12 strips dried are equal to 1 fresh stem; although 2–3 strips of very thinly peeled lemon zest will do just as well. Dried ground lemongrass is known as sereh powder in Indonesia. Also known as: *zabalin* (Burma), *kreung, bai mak nao* (Cambodia), *heung masu tso* (China), *sera* (India and Sri Lanka), *sereh* (Indonesia), *remon-sou* (Japan), *serai* (Malaysia), *takrai* (Thailand), *xa* (Vietnam).

Mace

Botanical name: *Myristica fragrans*

Mace is part of the nutmeg, a fruit that looks like an apricot and grows on tall tropical trees. When ripe, the fruit splits to reveal the aril, lacy and bright scarlet, surrounding the shell of the seed; the dried aril is mace and the kernel is nutmeg. Mace has a flavour similar to nutmeg but more delicate, and it is sometimes used in meat or fish curries, especially in Sri Lanka, although its main use in Asia is medicinal (a few blades of mace steeped in hot water, the water then being taken to combat nausea and diarrhoea). Also known as: *javatri* (India), *wasa-vasi* (Sri Lanka).

Maldive fish (Dried smoked tuna)

Dried tuna from the Maldive Islands is used extensively in Sri Lankan cooking. It is sold in packets, broken into small chips, but needs to be pulverised further using a mortar and pestle to make a powder before use. Substitute dried prawn (shrimp) powder or Japanese bonito flakes (katsuobushi). Also known as: *umbalakada* (Sri Lanka).

Miso

A paste made from cooked, fermented soy beans. There are various types: white, red, brownish and beige – with white and red being the main ones. There are also varying degrees of saltiness, so make sure you allow for it. Japanese thick soups are mostly based on miso stirred into dashi, the usual proportion being 1 tablespoon to 250 ml (8½ fl oz/1 cup) of stock. There is also a yellow bean paste used in Singapore and Indonesia called *taucheo*. *See salted soy beans (taucheo).*

Mushrooms, shiitake (dried)
Botanical name: *Lentinus edodes*

Also known as 'fragrant mushrooms', the flavour of these mushrooms is quite individual. They are expensive but give an incomparable flavour. Soak for 20–30 minutes before using. The stems are usually discarded and only the caps used. There is no substitute. Also known as: *hmo chauk* (Burma), *doong gwoo*, *leong goo* (China), *cindauwan* (Malaysia), *kabuteng shiitakena pinatuyo* (Philippines), *hed hom* (Thailand), *khô nm shiitake*, *nm ro'm khô* (Vietnam).

Mustard seeds, black
Botanical name: *Brassica nigra*

This variety of mustard seed is smaller and more pungent than the yellow variety. Substitute brown mustard seeds (*B. juncia*). Alba or white mustard seeds are not used in Asian cooking. Also known as: *rai*, *kimcea* (brown mustard) (India), *biji sawi* (Malaysia), *abba* (Sri Lanka).

Nutmeg
Botanical name: *Myristica fragrans*

Not widely used as a curry spice, but used to flavour some sweets and cakes, and sometimes used in garam masala. For maximum flavour, always grate finely just before using. Use sparingly, as large quantities (more than one whole nut) can be poisonous. Also known as: *zalipho thi* (Burma), *tau kau* (China), *jaiphal* (India), *pala* (Indonesia), *buah pala* (Malaysia), *sadikka* (Sri Lanka).

Palm sugar (jaggery)

This strong-flavoured dark sugar is obtained from the sap of coconut palms and Palmyrah palms. The sap is boiled down until it crystallises, and the sugar is usually sold in round, flat cakes or two hemispheres put together to form a ball and wrapped in dried leaves. Substitute black sugar, an unrefined, sticky sugar sold in health food stores, or use refined dark brown sugar sold at supermarkets. Thai recipes generally call for pale palm sugar, while Malaysian, Indonesian and Sri Lankan recipes favour dark palm sugar. Also known as: *jaggery*, *tanyet* (Burma), *skor tnowth* (Cambodia), *gur*, *jaggery* (India), *gula aren*, *gula jawa* (Indonesia), *gula Melaka* (Malaysia), *jaggery*, *hakuru* (Sri Lanka), *nam taan pep*, *nam taan bik*, *nam taan mapraow* (Thailand).

Pandanus or screwpine
Botanical name: *Pandanus latifolia*

Used as a flavouring in rice and curries in Sri Lanka, to wrap chicken for grilling or deep-frying in Thailand and Cambodia and as a flavouring and colouring agent in Malay and Indonesian sweets. The long, flat, green leaves are either crushed or boiled to yield up their flavour and colour. In Malaysia and Indonesia especially, the flavour is as popular as vanilla is in the West. It is available fresh and frozen in Asian grocery stores and increasingly common in good greengrocers. Also known as: *slok toey* (Cambodia), *daun pandan* (Indonesia and Malaysia), *rampe* (Sri Lanka), *bai toey* (Thailand).

Paprika
Botanical name: *Capsicum tetragonum*

Paprika peppers can be tinned or bottled as pimiento, but are more often used dried and powdered and known simply as paprika. Good paprika should have a mild, sweet flavour and brilliant red colour. Although it is essentially a European flavouring, particularly used in Hungary and Poland, it is useful in Asian cooking for imparting the necessary red colour to a curry when the chilli tolerance of the diners is not very high. In Asia, the colour would come from 20 to 30 chillies!

Peanut oil

A traditional cooking medium in Chinese and Southeast Asian countries. Asian unrefined peanut oil is highly flavoured and more expensive than the refined peanut oil found in Western supermarkets. It has a high smoking point and adds a distinctive flavour to stir-fries. Refined peanut oil is ideal for deep-frying. Take all the usual precautions where peanuts are concerned and avoid it if cooking for anyone with nut sensitivities. Use olive oil flavoured with a little sesame oil as an alternative.

Pepper, black
Botanical name: *Piper nigrum*

Pepper, the berry of a tropical vine native to India, is green when immature, and red or yellow when ripe. Black pepper is obtained by boiling and then sun-drying the green, unripe drupes. It is only used in some curries, but is an important ingredient in garam masala. Vietnam is the main producer of pepper. Also known as: *nga-youk-kaun* (Burma), *hu-chiao* (China), *kali mirich* (India), *merica hitam* (Indonesia), *kosho* (Japan), *phik noi* (Laos), *lada hitam* (Malaysia), *paminta* (Philippines), *gammiris* (Sri Lanka), *prik thai* (Thailand).

Prawn powder, dried

Finely shredded dried prawns (shrimp), sold in packets at speciality food stores and Asian grocery stores.

Red asian shallots
Botanical name: *Allium ascalonicum*

Shallots are small, purplish onions with red-brown skin. Like garlic, they grow in a cluster and resemble garlic cloves in shape. The name 'shallots' in Australia is generally (and incorrectly) given to spring onions in some states.

Rice, ground

This can be bought at supermarkets and health food stores. It is slightly more granular than rice flour. It gives a crisper texture when used in batters.

Rice vermicelli (rice-stick) noodles

These are very fine rice flour noodles sold in Chinese grocery stores. Soaking in hot water for 10 minutes prepares them sufficiently for most recipes, but in some cases they may need boiling for 1–2 minutes. When deep-fried they swell up and turn white. For a crisp result, fry them straight from the packet without soaking. Also known as: *mee sooer* (Cambodia), *mei fun* (China), *beehoon, meehoon* (Malaysia), *sen mee* (Thailand), *bún, lúa min* (Vietnam).

Rosewater
A favourite flavouring in Indian and Persian sweets, rosewater is the diluted essence extracted from rose petals by steam distillation. If you use rose essence or concentrate, be careful not to over-flavour and be sure to count the drops. However, with rosewater a 1 tablespoon-measure can safely be used. Buy rosewater from chemists or from shops specialising in Asian or Middle Eastern ingredients.

Roti flour
Creamy in colour and slightly granular in texture, this is ideal flour for all unleavened breads; unlike atta flour, it is not made from the whole grain but instead the polished or milled grain. Sold at some health food stores and Chinese grocery stores as well as Indian grocery stores.

Saffron
Botanical name: *Crocus sativus*
The world's most expensive spice, saffron is obtained by drying the stamens of the saffron or autumn crocus. The thread-like strands are dark orange in colour and have a strong perfume; it is also available in powder form. Do not confuse it with turmeric, which is sometimes sold as 'Indian saffron'. Beware also of cheap saffron, which in all probability will be safflower or 'bastard saffron' – it looks similar, and imparts colour, but has none of the saffron fragrance. Saffron is used more extensively in northern India than anywhere else in Asia. Also known as: *kesar* (China), *zaffran, kesari* (India), *koma-koma* (Malaysia), *kasubha* (Philippines).

Salted soy beans (taucheo)
An Indonesian or Malaysian fermented soy bean sauce. The beans may be whole, but are very soft and easy to mash. Yellow bean sauce is a smooth version. Thai soy bean paste is a suitable substitute. Also sold as *tauco* and *tauceo*.

Semolina
A wheat product sometimes known as 'farina', it comes in coarse, medium and fine grades. Recipes stipulate the correct grade to use, but a different grade can be substituted although there will be some change in texture. The bulk semolina sold in health food stores is medium grade; and the packaged semolina sold in Italian grocery stores and delicatessens is either medium or very fine. A little experimental shopping is recommended, for the grade of semolina is seldom labelled.

Sesame oil
The sesame oil used in Chinese cooking is extracted from toasted sesame seeds and gives a totally different flavour from the lighter-coloured sesame oil sold in health food stores. For the recipes in this book, buy sesame oil from Asian grocery stores. Use the oil in small quantities for flavouring, not as a cooking medium. Also known as: *hnan zi* (Burma), *ma yau* (China), *gingelly, til ka tel* (India), *goma abura* (Japan),

chan keh room (Korea), *minyak bijan* (Malaysia), *thala tel* (Sri Lanka), *dau me* (Vietnam).

Sesame seeds
Used mostly in Korean, Chinese and Japanese food, and in sweets in other Southeast Asian countries. Black sesame, another variety known as hak chih mah (China) or kuro goma (Japan), is mainly used in the Chinese dessert, toffee apples, and as a flavouring (gomashio) mixed with salt in Japanese food. Also known as: *hnan si* (Burma), *til, gingelly* (India), *wijen* (Indonesia), *keh* (Korea), *bijan* (Malaysia), *linga* (Philippines), *thala* (Sri Lanka), *nga dee la* (Thailand), *me* (Vietnam).

Shrimp paste, dried
Commercially sold as blacan, blachan or belacan, this is a pungent paste made from prawns (shrimp), and used in many Southeast Asian recipes. It is sold in tins, flat slabs or blocks and will keep indefinitely. If stored in an airtight jar it will, like a genie in a bottle, perform its magic when required without obtruding on the kitchen at other times! It does not need refrigeration. Also known as: *ngapi* (Burma), *trasi* (Indonesia), *blacan* (Malaysia), *kapi* (Thailand), *mam tom* (Vietnam).

Shrimp sauce
Although not widely distributed as *bagoong* (Philippines) or *petis* (Indonesia), this is sold at Asian grocery stores as 'shrimp sauce' or 'shrimp paste'. Thick and greyish in colour, with a powerful odour, it is one of the essential ingredients in the food of Southeast Asia. Substitute dried shrimp paste (blacan) or anchovy sauce.

Silver fungus
Also known as 'white wood fungus', this is so rare and expensive that it is used only in special festive dishes. Almost flavourless, it is prized for its crunchy texture and pretty appearance, and is also a 'prestige' food used to honour special guests. It is sold dried by the gram, or in tins cooked in a sweet syrup. However, the homemade version is infinitely preferable to the tinned silver fungus, which loses its texture through processing. Silver fungus is said to be very beneficial to pregnant women. Also known as: *sit gnee* (China), *shiro kikurage* (Japan), *cendawan jelly puteh* (Malaysia).

Soy sauce
Indispensable in Asian cooking, this versatile sauce enhances the flavour of every basic ingredient in a dish. Different grades are available. Chinese cooking uses light soy and dark soy. The light soy is used with chicken or seafoods, or in soups where the delicate colour of the dish must be retained. Always use shoyu (Japanese soy sauce) in Japanese cooking. In Indonesia, *kecap manis*, a thick, dark, sweetened soy, is often used. As a substitute, use dark Chinese soy with black or brown sugar added in the proportions given in recipes. All types of soy sauce keep indefinitely without refrigeration.

Spring onions (scallions)
Botanical name: *Allium cepa and fistulum*
Also known as green onions in some parts of the world, this member of the onion family is known as a 'shallot' in some

areas of Australia, but is correctly called a spring onion almost everywhere else – although the term 'scallion' is popular in the United States. Spring onions are the thinnings of either *Allium cepa* or *A. fistulum* plantings that do not form a bulb. They are white and slender with green leaves, and are used widely in China and Japan. Also known as: *da cong, tai tsung* (China), *hari piaz* (India), *daun bawang* (Indonesia), *negi* (Japan), *phak boua sot* (Laos), *daun bawang* (Malaysia), *sibuyas na tagsibol* (Philippines), *ton hom* (Thailand), *hanh la* (Vietnam).

Spring roll pastry
Thin, white sheets of pliable pastry sold in plastic packets and kept frozen. Thaw and peel off one at a time (unused wrappers can be re-frozen). Large wrappers of the won ton type cannot be substituted.

Star Anise
Botanical name: *Illicium verum*
The dried, star-shaped fruit of an evergreen tree native to China and Vietnam, it usually consists of eight segments or points. It is essential in Chinese cooking and is one of the key flavours in the stock for the Vietnamese rice noodle soup, *pho*. Also known as: *baht gok* (China), *badian* (India), *bunga lawang* (Indonesia and Malaysia), *poy kak bua* (Thailand), *hoi* (Vietnam).

Tamarind
Botanical name: *Tamarindus indica*
The tamarind is a sour-tasting fruit of a large tropical tree. It is shaped like a large broad (fava) bean and has a brittle brown shell, inside which are shiny dark seeds covered with tangy brown flesh. Tamarind is dried into a pulp and sold in packets, as well as diluted with water and sold as a purée. These can vary in concentration. The pulp needs to be soaked first in hot water, then squeezed until it breaks up and dissolves. It needs to be strained before using. May be substituted with lemon juice. Also known as: *ma-gyi-thi* (Burma), *ampil tum* (ripe), *ampil kheei* (green) (Cambodia), *imli* (India), *mal kham* (Laos), *asam* (Malaysia and Indonesia), *sampalok* (Philippines), *siyambala* (Sri Lanka), *som ma kham* (Thailand), *me* (Vietnam).

Taucheo
See salted soy beans.

Turmeric
Botanical name: *Curcuma longa*
A rhizome of the ginger family, turmeric, with its orange-yellow colour, is a mainstay of commercial curry powders. Though often called Indian saffron, it should never be confused with true saffron and the two may not be used interchangeably. Also known as: *fa nwin, sa nwin* (Burma), *romiet* (Cambodia), *wong geung fun* (China), *haldi* (India), *kunyit* (Indonesia), *ukon* (Japan), *kunyit* (Malaysia), *dilau* (Philippines), *kaha* (Sri Lanka), *khamin* (Thailand), *cú nghê, ngh* (Vietnam).

Winter bamboo shoots
See bamboo shoots.

Glossary

INDEX

Index ◆